EUROPA ✠ MILITARIA 1.

WORLD WAR I
INFANTRY

IN COLOUR PHOTOGRAPHS

LAURENT MIROUZE

Windrow & Greene
London

BELGIAN INFANTRYMAN, AUGUST 1914

The small Belgian army resisted the first German offensive valiantly; but heroic resistance could not outweigh the massive advantage in numbers and resources enjoyed by the invaders.

The silhouette of the Belgian infantryman of 1914 was one of the most archaic in Western Europe; the felt shako, heavy greatcoat, large ventral cartridge pouch and enormous pack contributed to his generally old-fashioned appearance. As in neighbouring France, the high command had been slow to modernise the army; and it was unfortunate that the first of the planned reforms of uniform and equipment were interrupted by the outbreak of hostilities. It immediately became evident that the Belgian soldier's outfit was badly adapted to modern warfare, and the first changes were forced through after a matter of weeks; these involved a general simplification, dictated as much by economy as by battlefield conditions.

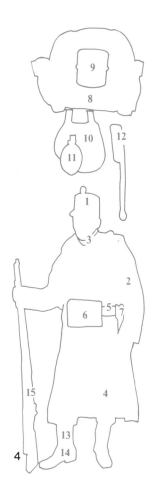

1—Black felt shako, its brass plate bearing a central regimental number; in campaign dress it was covered with this black oilcloth sleeve with a white-painted number, here that of the 9th Line Infantry. The broad chinstrap and red woollen pompon contributed to the shako's 19th century appearance.

2—Greatcoat of heavy cloth, in a shade known as '*gros bleu*'. It had a turned-down collar, and fastened by two rows of five brass buttons bearing the regimental number. On each side a brass hook helped support the weight of the belt kit; and there were two large side pockets with single-button flaps. The rear vent could be closed by two buttons; a two-button integral half-belt adjusted the fit at the rear waist; and the skirts could be buttoned back to free the legs on the march. Obscured by the coat in these photos is a *veste* of similar colour, fastened by a single row of six buttons. The button-cyphers are the only indication of the unit.

3—Black satin stock edged with leather, protecting the neck from the chafing of the greatcoat.

4—Heavy grey-blue cloth trousers, cut straight, with vertical slash side pockets; an integral rear half-belt adjusted the fit at the waist.

5—Black leather belt; the rectangular brass buckle plate, obscured here, was worn slightly to the left of centre because of the position of the pouch.

6—Black leather cartridge pouch, its flap fastened at the rear by two brass studs. Two rear hooks engaged with the front braces of the knapsack, as illustrated.

7—Black leather bayonet frog with hilt strap. The bayonet scabbard was often seen slung above the entrenching tool, with the strap of the tool carrier holding the scabbard steady, in the German fashion.

8—Knapsack of cow hide, edged with black leather and lined with grey cloth, and with a compartmented cane framework. It contained changes of clothes and reserve rations. Four exterior straps allowed stowage of the bedroll and spare boots.

9—Black-painted aluminium mess tin, inspired by the German pattern; it contained a spoon which doubled as a handle. It fixed to the knapsack flap by means of a black strap.

10—Brown cloth haversack, with leather belt loops; it had three internal pockets, and a strap and ring on the flap for the attachment of the water bottle. The haversack could be worn slung round the body on a cloth strap, if wished.

11—Water bottle in aluminium covered with khaki cloth, fitted with a hook on a neck strap. Of one litre capacity, the water bottle too resembled contemporary German issue.

12—Entrenching tool, Linnemann pattern, carried from the belt by means of a black leather frame with two straps.

13—Black leather gaiters, laced up the front by means of metal hooks.

14—Standard issue boots of blackened leather.

15—Mauser M1889 rifle of 7.65mm calibre.

GERMAN INFANTRYMAN, AUGUST 1914

This senior corporal of Infantry Regiment 'Herwarth von Bittenfeld' (1st Westphalian) No.13 represents the classic German soldier of popular imagination. Although he has recently been equipped with a modern uniform of neutral *Feldgrau* colour, he retains certain elements handed down through a long military tradition, which still recall the war of 1870-71.

The spiked helmet and the knee-length marching boots had been in use for generations in the Prussian, and later the German army, and had an old-fashioned look in the second decade of the 20th century. Nevertheless, the iron discipline of the Kaiser's army, and its excellent equipment—particularly the formidable MG08 machine gun, which decimated the French infantry of 1914—quickly dispelled any illusions about Germany's readiness for war.

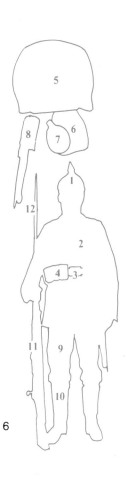

1—M1895 *Pickelhaube* helmet, the latest in a series of similar helmets stretching back to 1842. It was made of boiled leather, with brass spike and fittings, and offered little protection. On campaign the M1892 helmet cover, with a simple applied cloth regimental number in red, concealed the helmet's frontal plate —which varied according to the regiment—and the side cockades, of which one was in the Imperial colours and one in the colours of the *Land* or state of origin.

2—M1907/10 tunic in 'field grey' cloth, fastening with a single row of eight buttons whose metal and design varied according to the regiment. Most infantry regiments had the turned-down collar, the front edge, and the simulated three-button pocket flaps in the tails piped red. The cuff flaps varied in design according to unit, but often, as here, were of 'Brandenburg' shape, and ornamented with three buttons. This NCO's status is marked by gold braid round the collar and cuffs. The field grey shoulder straps were detachable; they were piped in colours identifying the army corps to which the regiment belonged, and bore a red number or monogram identifying the regiment.

3—M1895 belt in tan leather, flesh side out; the buckle plate varied according to the *Land*—here it is Prussian, in brass with a white metal central cartouche bearing the Prussian crown and the motto '*Gott Mit Uns*'—'God With Us'.

4—M1909 cartridge pouches in pebbled-finish brown leather. Each of the six pouches, in two sets of three, holds four five-round clips of 7.92mm cartridges, giving a total of 120 rounds. The weight is distributed by means of a ring mounted behind each triple pouch, hooking to the front brace of the knapsack.

5—M1895 knapsack in cow hide, the flap faced with unshaven hide; all leather parts are brown, and the pack has a wooden internal frame. The knapsack accommodated changes of clothes, blankets, off-duty footwear, reserve rations, etc. The outer stowage comprised the grey M1907 greatcoat and the M1892 beige-coloured tent cloth. The M1910 mess tin in black-painted aluminium was fixed to the pack flap by two brown straps.

6—M1887 haversack, popularly called the 'bread-bag', made of light brown cloth; it looped to the belt by two buttoned cloth straps and a central metal hook. Two rings on the inner face allowed the attachment of a sling so that it could also be worn slung round the body. The haversack accommodated rations and eating utensils as well as small personal effects.

7—The M1907 water bottle of cloth-covered aluminium, hooked to the haversack.

8—M1887 entrenching tool, looped to the left of the belt by a leather carrier; the lower straps also secured the bayonet scabbard to the spade handle—this scabbard is the M1898 in steel-reinforced leather. The bayonet knot is the NCO's silver thread pattern.

9—M1907/10 trousers in field grey, with red piping down the outer seams; these had two diagonal side slash pockets and a small frontal fob pocket, and an integral rear half-belt for waist adjustment.

10—M1866 tan leather marching boots, flesh side out.

11—M1898 Mauser rifle, 7.92mm calibre.

12—M1898 bayonet; theoretically, NCOs were supposed to be issued with a special pattern with a saw-toothed back edge.

FRENCH INFANTRYMAN, AUGUST 1914

The unsuitability of the French infantryman's uniform for modern warfare came as no surprise in 1914. Since the Boer War of 1899-1902 had demonstrated to the world the importance of drab field uniform, French reformers had been pressing for a radical modification of issue clothing, as much of the cut as the colours. Between 1903 and 1914 many trials were carried out with experimental uniforms of drab, grey-blue, beige-blue and reseda-green, but none were taken into service; ironically, a decision was finally taken on 27 July 1914, just six days before the outbreak of war. The French infantryman suffered through the first months in a uniform which had hardly changed since the Franco-Prussian War. Sent against German machine guns in mad bayonet charges, the 'red trousers' fell like corn before the scythe, until the miraculous rally before the Marne.

1—M1884 *képi,* with dark blue band and red top, rounded visor and chinstrap of black leather, and regimental number applied to the band in red cut-out digits. The blue cloth campaign cover was the sole concession to modern military conditions, and dated from 1913.

2—Blue cotton stock, knotted like a cravat.

3—M1877 greatcoat in heavy cloth of the shade known as 'blued-iron grey'. Hardly changed since the Second Empire, it was double-breasted, with two rows of six half-ball buttons of yellow metal bearing a grenade device. There was an integral rear half-belt for waist adjustment, and two rear pockets with access via the long central vent. The skirts could be buttoned back on campaign, and buttoned rear vents allowed the cuffs to be turned up. The low, uncomfortable standing collar bore red patches, with the regimental number sewn on in cut-out digits made from coat cloth. This man has the two large red diagonal cuff stripes of a corporal. The shoulders have detachable rolled shoulder straps, M1913, to stop the slings of the equipment slipping off.

4—Lebel rifle equipment in black leather, flesh side out, which incorporated the old belt with its brass buckle plate, and comprised:
— Three M1888 or M1905 cartridge pouches (differing only in the design of the rear belt loops).
— Y-shaped M1892 brace system, fixed to the back of each of the three pouches by a brass hook.
— M1888 frog for the Lebel's needle bayonet; this was looped to the left of the belt, but it and the blackened bronze scabbard are completely obscured here by the haversack and the coat turn-back.

5—M1893 knapsack with shoulder straps and stowage straps, all of black leather, and a rigid wooden internal frame; this pack had hardly changed since the days of Louis Napoleon. In August 1914 the exterior stowage no longer included blankets or tent cloth, but was limited to a pair of off-duty shoes in a bag, and the M1852 mess tin—slightly tilted, to allow the soldier's head back in the prone firing position; an individual tool on the left side—here the Seurre M1909 pick/shovel; and one of the squad's pieces of camping equipment. Rather than the large dixie or the flat pan, this man carries the big loaf of bread which represented a squad's daily ration.

6—M1892 haversack in beige cloth, containing daily rations, eating utensils, and—in theory—the mug, which in practice was usually slung to the water bottle strap.

7—One-litre M1877 water bottle with two spouts, made of tinned iron and covered with old coat cloth; it was normally carried slung on the right hip, and the haversack on the left.

8—Red cloth trousers, M1867 modified in 1893 and 1897; the changes had been minimal. The straight-cut trousers had a pocket in each side seam and one right frontal pocket, and a rear half-belt for adjustment.

9—M1913 gaiters in black leather, lacing up the front by means of hooks and eyelets; these were adopted after numerous experimental examples were tried, beginning in 1897.

10—Black leather ankle boots. Various different models were in use in 1914, principally the high-topped *brodequin* with six pairs of eyelets, adopted in 1893. The more recent 1912 pattern had a lower top and seven pairs of eyelets; this was similar to that shown here, but without the reinforcing rivet at the side of the instep, which did not reappear until 1916.

11—M1886/93 Lebel rifle of 8mm calibre; this bolt-action weapon utilised the out-dated Kropatschek system, with eight cartridges accomodated in a tubular magazine under the barrel. The M1886 cruciform needle bayonet had a 'German silver' hilt and a recurved quillon.

François Vauvillier

BRITISH INFANTRYMAN, AUGUST 1914

On the eve of the Great War the British Army was extremely well equipped and well armed. The lessons of the most recent colonial campaigns had been learned—particularly those taught at such murderous cost by the South African Boers in 1899-1902. The most obvious reform was the adoption of a simple, practical and inconspicuous uniform of khaki cloth. The personal equipment was innovative in both its material and its design. The former was the strong cotton webbing first seen in the 1880s, when Capt. Anson Mills of the US Army used it for improved cartridge belts; the various equipment items were now arranged in an integrated system giving reasonable distribution of weight. The soldier's personal weapon was also well adapted for modern warfare: the Short Magazine Lee Enfield rifle No.1 Mark III of .303in. calibre, with a ten-round removable box magazine allowing sustained rapid fire. Despite their small numbers, the British Expeditionary Force put up bloody resistance to the German divisions which poured into Belgium and northern France in the summer of 1914.

1—M1905 service dress cap in khaki serge, lined with black oilskin. The rigid visor was covered with khaki cloth; and there was a narrow leather chinstrap fixed by two small uniform buttons. The metal cap badge varied from regiment to regiment; here it is the brass grenade device of the Grenadier Guards, the army's senior regiment of foot.

2—M1902 service dress tunic in khaki serge, of simple and practical cut, which hardly changed until 1937. The turned-down collar was fixed by one or two hooks and eyes. There were four front pockets with straight buttoned flaps, the chest pockets being pleated. The shoulders were reinforced against the weight and chafing of the equipment with rectangular cloth patches. There were two short rear vents behind the hips. The only unit insignia worn on the tunic at this date were the regimental titles—brass lettering spelling out abbreviated forms of the regimental name—worn on the ends of the shoulder straps. In this example we see the alternative style peculiar to the Brigade of Guards—woven titles in white on red cloth, sewn to the top of the sleeves.

3—M1902 service dress trousers in khaki serge. These straight-cut trousers had two vertical slash side pockets; they were worn with braces, and had 12 buttons arranged round the waist.

4—M1908 cotton webbing equipment, carrying all the soldier's field necessities by means of an interconnected system adjusted by buckled straps; it could be put on or taken off in one piece by unfastening the belt. The separate items could be arranged in a number of different ways; the arrangement illustrated is the 'marching order' for the rifleman.

On the left hip is the haversack, containing rations, eating utensils, and personal effects. Under this are the bayonet scabbard, with the entrenching tool helve attached to it by straps. On the right hip are the entrenching tool head in its carrier, beneath the water bottle of two pints capacity, made of enamelled steel covered with khaki cloth. On the front of the body, left and right, are two sets each of five cartridge pouches; each pouch accomodated three five-round charger clips, giving a load of 150 rounds in all. Attached to the shoulder braces and to diagonal straps projecting backwards from the cartridge pouch sets is the pack or 'valise', containing the greatcoat, changes of clothing, etc.; the long diagonal straps allowed exterior stowage. The whole set was based upon a broad waist belt, and broad shoulder braces crossing on the back.

5—M1902 khaki cloth puttees, secured by tapes.

6—'Ammunition boots', blackened for service dress but often unblackened and greased for field use.

7—Short Magazine Lee Enfield rifle No.1 Mark III, calibre .303in.; this bolt-action rifle, in the hands of the long-service regulars of the first BEF, was capable of very rapid, accurate fire, and was a byword for sturdiness and reliability.

8—M1908 webbing sling.

RUSSIAN INFANTRYMAN, AUGUST 1914

The Russo-Japanese War of 1904-05 had ended in disaster for the Imperial Russian army, and the necessity of reforming the uniforms and equipment issued to the Tsar's troops was clear. Nicholas II took a personal interest in the problem; and by the outbreak of the Great War the long-suffering Russian infantryman had been re-equipped with a much more practical outfit and lightened field equipment. Some elements of this uniform and equipment can still be recognised, in developed form, among today's Soviet soldiers. The regulations accompanying the new uniform (which was khaki from 1908) provided for a military version of the traditional Russian shirt-tunic, the 'gymnastiorka'; trousers cut like semi-breeches; and a visored cap badged with a cockade in the Romanov colours. A heavier version of the same basic uniform was issued for cold weather. The soft leather knee-boots and 'horseshoe' roll completed the typical image of the Russian soldier.

1—M1907/10 cap in cotton or linen, of a light khaki shade, with a leather visor. Leather chinstraps were not regulation, but were often added. On the front of the band was a pressed tin cockade painted in the orange and black Imperial colours.

2—M1912 'gymnastiorka', a long, baggy shirt-tunic traditionally worn by the Russian peasantry, here in light khaki cotton; a woollen version was issued for winter. The stand collar fastened with two small off-set buttons. This 'pullover' garment had a front vent from collar to mid-chest only, fastened by two or three small buttons. There were many variations of detail, given the dispersed manufacture of uniforms —typical differences included chest pockets, gathered cuffs, button placing on the collar or chest, etc. The characteristic shoulder straps were rigid, removable 'shoulder boards' in uniform colour bearing the number or monogram of the unit.

3—M1907 semi-breeches, cut full in the thigh and tight at the knee, and made in khaki-green cotton or wool depending on the season. There were two vertical side pockets.

4—The trousers tucked into black leather knee-boots, which were worn by all ranks and categories of troops apart from certain specialists such as bicycle units. They are still worn today, virtually unchanged.

5—Tent cloth and greatcoat, rolled together and worn in a 'horseshoe' round the body. The M1911 greatcoat was a straight, single-breasted garment fastened by five brass front buttons charged with the Imperial eagle; it had straight cuffs, and an integral rear half-belt with two adjustment buttons. The tent section rolled round it here is of khaki material.

6—The ends of the tent/greatcoat roll were strapped tightly together and stuffed into the open M1909 mess tin, which was made of copper alloy.

7—M1909 aluminium water bottle covered with khaki cloth. The soldier's mug was strapped to the bottom of the bottle; and the assembly was slung round the body on a leather strap.

8—Leather belt, with a brass buckle plate charged with the two-headed Imperial eagle, of the type adopted in 1904.

9—M1893 brown leather cartridge pouches; each of the pair accomodated six five-round charger-clips, giving a total load of 60 rounds of rifle ammunition.

10—'Linnemann'-type entrenching tool, here in a leather carrier; the tool itself remained unchanged up to the Second World War, but the carrier was made in various materials, often in fabric.

11—M1910 haversack; the bag was made of greyish-beige waterproofed cloth, the straps of leather. It was normally worn slung round the body, but the sling could be arranged in such a way that it could be worn on the back like a knapsack. The usual contents were rations, minimal changes of clothing, such as the foot-cloths wrapped round the feet inside the boots, small personal effects, and 40 more cartridges.

12—M1891 Mosin Nagant rifle, calibre 7.62mm, of the model known as 'three-line'. The long socket bayonet, M1891, was carried permanently fixed; the rifle sling was of leather.

SCOTTISH INFANTRYMAN, SEPTEMBER 1914

The Scottish Highland infantryman was perhaps the most visually striking of all the Western European soldiers who went to war in 1914. The same loyalty to tradition which made him such a formidable fighting man had preserved elements of his traditional national costume—most noticeably the Glengarry bonnet with its diced band, and the kilt. Only the Highland units—traditionally, but by now not exclusively recruited in the hills of northern and western Scotland—retained the kilt. In 1914 there were five regiments each of two battalions, which were distinguished one from the other by differences in the Glengarry, kilt and hose-tops; the rest of the uniform was almost identical to that of the other British infantry regiments. The uniform illustrated is that of the Seaforth Highlanders, whose 2nd Battalion was one of eight Highland battalions which went to France in August 1914 with the BEF.

1—The Glengarry had been adopted by the whole infantry in the 1860s as undress headgear. In most Scottish regiments it was retained in place of the service dress cap, the use or absence of variously diced bands identifying different units. The Seaforths wore the usual dark blue ribboned bonnet, with a red pompon, a band diced in red, white and blue, and the regimental badge on a silk backing.

2—M1902 service dress tunic, of the 'doublet' cut issued to Scottish regiments, with the front skirts cut away and rounded; the standard tunic was often issued instead as the war progressed, and retailored at unit level. The only insignia worn in 1914 were the brass shoulder titles on the shoulder straps.

3—M1908 khaki webbing equipment, as described on p.10. The assembly of this 'marching order' was as follows:
- The bayonet frog was slid onto the belt on the left hip; the webbing entrenching tool helve holder was buckled to it with two straps. The left and right pouch sets were then looped to the front of the belt.
- Two shoulder braces were buckled to the upper rear of the pouch sets, leaving a length of webbing falling behind the set and protruding under the belt. The braces passed over the shoulders, crossed in the middle of the back, and passed through buckles on the back of the belt. This left four brace ends hanging below the belt, at left front and back and right front and back.
- To the two ends hanging on the right the entrenching tool head carrier was buckled, the ends of the braces engaging with the water bottle carrier which hung over the tool head carrier.
- To the two ends hanging on the left the haversack was buckled, hanging on the left hip over the bayonet and tool helve.
- The 'valise' (knapsack) was attached by two buckles to the upper rear of the shoulder braces. Two narrow diagonal straps passing backwards round the body from the rear of the ammunition pouch sets engaged with the buckles of the two external pack straps, which were anchored by loops under the valise

at each side; and these external straps then passed up and across the pack to buckles on its inner top surface. The whole weight of the ammunition, belt kit and pack was thus distributed as evenly as possible.

4—The kilt, a length of woollen cloth about seven yards long but arranged in 'accordion pleats' except at the two ends, wound round the waist so as to leave the unpleated part at the front, and secured with two buckled straps at the side. Each regiment had its own distinctive tartan, in the case of the Seaforths the Mackenzie sett; but all units on campaign wore covered kilts.

5—The kilt cover, a light brown drab apron which completely obscured the colourful tartan of the kilt, and which fastened by buckles on the right. In front a large flapped pocket replaced the sporran of full and walking-out dress, which was never worn on campaign.

6—In 1914 the men of each kilted regiment could also be distinguished by the particular pattern of their checkered woollen 'hose-tops'. These were replaced more or less at once by khaki stockings.

7—The hose-tops or stockings were held up by garters, with visible flashes of different shapes and colours depending on the unit.

8—Heavy cloth gaiters, of the old 'spatterdash' shape, covered the stockings and boots at the beginning of the war; they were soon replaced by short puttees. The gaiters had eight small side buttons and a leather strap under the instep.

9—Hobnailed 'ammunition boots'.

10—SMLE rifle No.1 Mark III, calibre .303in.

FRENCH INFANTRYMAN, SPRING 1915

In the aftermath of the battle of the Marne, France more than any other country faced the urgent necessity of re-equipping her army for a war which was evidently going to last much longer than had been imagined. A new uniform colour, symbolically termed 'tricolour cloth' and woven of a mixture of red, white and blue threads, had been chosen a few days before the outbreak of war, but never issued. Ironically, it turned out that all the dyes—even the famous '*garance*' red—were obtained from Germany; and France was reduced to seizing the stocks of a French subsidiary of a German company. Indigo blue was readily available, but not alizarine red ('*garance*'). Thus the new weave was reduced to two colours, blue and white; and thus, by the chances of war, was born the light blue shade which passed into history as 'horizon blue'.

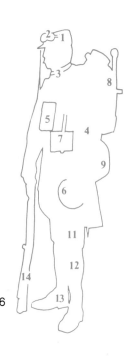

1—M1914 *képi*, a simplified version of the traditional shape. The cloth used in this example is 'English blue-grey', an imported fabric used in 1914-15 to supplement hard-pressed French resources.

2—Anti-gas goggles; many varying models were used from May 1915 onwards.

3—The blue cotton stock; also just visible is the collar of the pre-war dark blue *veste*, a nine-button 'stable jacket' with red collar patches bearing dark blue regimental numbers.

4—M1914 simplified greatcoat in 'horizon blue'. To cut both cost and delivery time the leading designer of the day, Paul Poiret, produced in September 1914 this single-breasted pattern with six front buttons. The large falling collar bears the yellow patches with dark blue regimental numbers and pipings introduced for the infantry by regulations of 9 December 1914. Some coats had two breast pockets with buttoned flaps, some only one on the right side, as here. Buttons were initially of simple four-hole design; the old pattern charged with a grenade device were later revived, but in white metal painted grey-blue. The dark blue star on the left arm is a non-regulation badge worn by infantry scouts.

5—Anti-gas sachet, here the very first model—the 'Compress C1', issued in May 1915. The sachet, tied by a tape to the coat button, was made of rubberised cloth; it contained a pad of cotton impregnated with hyposulphite and carbonate of soda, which the soldier was supposed to clap over his nose and mouth like a modern 'smog mask' in case of gas alert.

6—Steel skull protector. Although in some ways slow to modernise, the French army was the first to adopt any kind of head protection. From March 1915 a 'brain pan' recalling the 17th century '*cervelière*' was issued for wear under the *képi*. This unpopular device was only a hasty stop-gap until the issue of a true helmet, which had been decided upon in February 1915.

7—Lebel rifle equipment. This was essentially unchanged since August 1914, apart from the issue of the new M1903 belt with a two-prong buckle.

8—Campaign pack. Throughout the war the French infantryman would retain the basic pack issued at the outbreak of hostilities, by now completely out-of-date. From the end of 1914 onward his burden was increased by the addition to the knapsack of rolled blankets and a tent section, complete with its pegs and cords. The knapsack illustrated here is a simplified model of wartime manufacture, in grey-blue fabric. An item from the squad's campaign equipment (here, a folding canvas bucket) and an individual tool (here, the M1879 portable spade) are attached to the pack in regulation manner; the brown leather carrier for the spade indicates 1915 manufacture.

9—M1892 haversack, here a wartime-made example in greenish grey fabric.

10—M1877 one-litre water bottle, covered in old grey-blue coat cloth.

11—M1914 trousers of *pantalon-culotte* style, loose in the thigh and tight from the knee down, to be worn with puttees. Examples manufactured in late 1914 and early 1915 were often made of coarse corduroy in various drab shades—horizon blue cloth was at that time reserved for *képis* and greatcoats. Theoretically these trousers should have been worn under the blue overalls issued since 1914 to conceal the old red trousers, but issue was erratic.

12—Puttees in neutral drab cloth; long the mark of the Chasseurs Alpins, these became general issue for foot troops at the end of 1914.

13—M1912 boots, lacking the reinforcement rivet at the side.

14—M1886/93 Lebel rifle, 8mm calibre, and its bayonet.

François Vauvillier

17

GERMAN INFANTRYMAN, WESTERN FRONT, APRIL 1915

When the advances of summer 1914 ground to a halt, and the front lines stabilised for what threatened to be a long war, the German army was forced to reconsider an elaborate uniform which had been devised in peacetime. The huge numbers of men deployed and their lavish consumption of all kinds of stores took the German commissariat by surprise, and stockpiles diminished at alarming rates. The Allied maritime blockade of the Central Powers also created shortages of raw materials from 1915 on; and German industry was obliged to apply its ingenuity to the production of synthetic and substitute materials—the famous '*ersatz*' products which gave the world a new term.

At the level of the fighting soldiers the most immediate result was the steady replacement of leather by vulcanised fibre, of brass by painted iron, and of uniforms of pre-war quality by simplified designs made of inferior material. The appearance of the German infantryman had already begun to change by the end of the first year of the war.

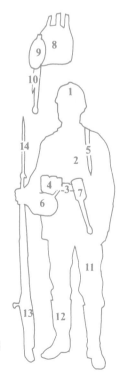

1—M1915 helmet, the last of the spiked *Pickelhaube* series, soon to be replaced by a new steel design. In most cases the skull of this helmet remained in boiled leather, but there were also examples made of felt, of compressed cardboard, and of thin metal (which offered no serious protection). The helmet fittings were in all cases of white metal alloy painted grey. The spike, judged to be too obviously visible, was now removed on campaign by means of a socket fixing. The cloth helmet cover therefore lost its own point; and, also for reasons of concealment, its red regimental numbers.

2—M1914 tunic, a simplified version of the M1907/10. The cut was more close-fitting; the tone of the field grey cloth became rather darker and greener; and the fancy cuff patches and false skirt pocket flaps were omitted. The cuffs themselves became deeper; but the NCO braid was now displayed only on the collar. The shoulder straps of field grey cloth were now piped in white for all infantry formations, with unit numbers or monograms embroidered in red; the straps were now sewn down at the shoulder seams. The black and white ribbon worn in the second tunic buttonhole marks an award of the Iron Cross 2nd Class.

3—M1895 belt, now blackened, and with an iron buckle plate painted field grey; older two-metal buckle plates still in use were similarly painted over.

4—M1909 cartridge pouches; the new regulations called for them to be blackened, but the nature of the leather used made this difficult to achieve consistently.

5—The soldier illustrated wears lightened field equipment, without the cumbersome M1895 knapsack. The considerable weight of the cartridge pouches with a full load of 120 rounds led to the use of the 'breadbag' sling as a neck brace in the absence of the knapsack's forward braces.

6—M1915 gasmask; the '*Gummimaske*' comprised a mask of rubberised fabric and a detachable filter cartridge, which were carried (with a spare cartridge) in a strong cloth bag looped to the belt.

7—M1915 'stick' hand grenade.

8—M1887 'breadbag', in this case a wartime example in poor quality grey fabric.

9—M1907 water bottle, also of '*ersatz*' manufacture, in enamelled iron here covered with brown corduroy, probably of civilian origin. The attachment strap system was reduced to its simplest form.

10—M1887 entrenching spade in its leather carrier, secured to the scabbard of the M1898/1905 bayonet by a strap.

11—M1914 trousers; these were identical in cut and pocket details to the M1907/10 pattern, but made of a 'stone grey' cloth—*Steingrau*. This was chosen when it was discovered that the *Feldgrau* trousers rapidly faded in use; this darker shade lasted longer. The red piping down the outer seams was retained.

12—M1866 marching boots in tan leather; these were ordered to be blackened in 1915.

13—M1898 Mauser rifle, 7.92mm calibre.

14—M1898/1905 bayonet. Originally introduced for the foot artillery, with a leather scabbard, it was issued from 1915 to the whole infantry arm with a sturdier metal scabbard, replacing the longer and more fragile M1898 infantry bayonet.

18

19

ITALIAN LIGHT INFANTRYMAN, ITALIAN FRONT, 1915

Like most European armies, the Italians put in hand a radical reform of field uniforms at the beginning of the 20th century. At that date Italy was allied to the Austro-Hungarian Empire and Germany, and the influence of the latter——after her prestigious victory of 1870-71—was considerable. In 1909 Italy adopted, like Austria-Hungary, a uniform colour similar to the German *Feldgrau* of 1907; in Italy's case this was termed simply '*grigio-verde*', 'grey-green'. A grey-green shade was also chosen for leather equipment from 1907 onwards.

The light infantry or '*Bersaglieri*', founded by Captain Alessandro La Marmora in 1836, were a *corps d'élite*. These light infantry units were repeatedly deployed during Italy's various 19th century campaigns, and acquired a reputation for dash, courage, and practical experience. During the Great War they were credited with turning the tide in Italy's favour in many battles. Their traditional undress headgear, inherited from Crimean campaigns alongside the Turks, was a crimson fez with a blue tassel.

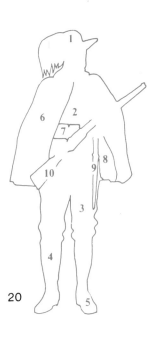

1—M1871 hat, of pressed felt and simulated leather, with black-green cock's-feather plumes on the right side; this headgear was peculiar to the *Bersaglieri*. The frontal cockade in red, white and green bore a stamped brass badge in the shape of a flaming 'grenade' bearing the regimental number, and crossed rifles. On campaign the hat was fitted with a grey cloth cover bearing the badge embroidered in black on a grey-green background. The hat was, of course, unsuitable for modern warfare, and was later replaced by the M1916 steel helmet; this, too, was fitted with the *Bersaglieri* plumes.

2—M1909 tunic in *grigio-verde*, with a standing collar and a fly front. There were no visible external pockets. The cuffs were pointed, and there were two short rear vents which fastened with a button. Although obscured here, the collar patches were crimson, bearing the star of Savoy worn by all Italian soldiers.

3—M1909 trousers; these were laced at the ankles, and had two diagonal side pockets.

4—M1909 puttees, which replaced the old black gaiters previously worn at the time of the outbreak of war.

5—M1912 ankle boots in brown leather; these were provided with cleats for mountain use.

6—M1912 cape. This short grey-green cape was issued to all infantry at the outbreak of the war. It had a falling collar fastened with a hook, and bearing the ubiquitous star of Savoy; a hidden button fastened the chest.

7—M1907 personal equipment, made of leather which was chemically treated to give a greyish colour. The belt had a simple one-prong buckle; unusually, the brace to support the weight of the belt kit was not the 'Y' or 'X' arrangement favoured in other armies, but a single loop passing round the neck and down the front again. There was a matching bayonet frog; and a pair of double cartridge pouches for the Carcano 6.5mm ammunition.

8—M1907 haversack. This was made of heavy cloth with leather fittings and could be arranged either as a knapsack or as a haversack, as in our illustrations. It accommodated all the soldier's immediate necessities.

9—M1891 bayonet.

10—M1891 Carcano carbine, 6.5mm calibre—this was the Italian army's standard calibre. The carbine was originally designed as a cavalry weapon, but was later issued to all light troops. It had a permanently fixed folding bayonet.

21

BRITISH INFANTRYMAN, WESTERN FRONT, OCTOBER 1915

After the retreat from Mons, the harsh winter of 1914-15 found the combatants of both sides holding stabilised front lines; there now began the long agony of trench warfare, which would last until well into 1918. Like the other armies, the British discovered that their issue clothing and equipment needed adaptation to the new realities of positional warfare, under increasingly heavy artillery fire, in all weathers.

A new army of volunteers was raised in Britain, to replace the very serious losses suffered by the first BEF (up to 90% in most battalions committed to the early campaigns). The unexpected demand for uniforms and equipment forced many of these volunteers of 'Kitchener's army' to train in civilian clothing; stocks intended for training had already been rushed to the front, where the Regulars improvised as best they could, and gratefully received the goatskin winter jerkins which made them look like soldiers in the Crimea. The rigid service dress cap now gave way to a soft model with let-down ear and neck flaps, giving better protection against cold. The smart silhouette of 1914 was already changing under pressure of trench conditions.

1—M1915 trench cap, popularly known as the 'Gor 'blimey', possibly in reference to the reaction of Regular NCOs to its unsoldierly appearance. Essentially similar to the rigid version, it had a soft visor and unstiffened crown, and deep neck and ear flaps which buttoned round the face in bad weather, and were turned up and buttoned over the crown when not in use. There was no chinstrap. Regimental badges were, as before, worn on the band; this is that of the King's Royal Rifle Corps, on its regimental scarlet cloth backing patch.

2—M1902 service dress tunic. For Rifle regiments all badges and buttons were black; note the 'KRR' regimental title on the shoulder straps. The rifle marksman's skill-at-arms badge on the left cuff is in brass, however.

3—'PH' type anti-gas hood in its small two-button satchel. Rushed into service after heavy casualties under gas attack at Ypres on 22-23 April 1915, the phenate-hexamine hood of flannel lined with cotton was impregnated with these chemicals, which supposedly neutralised the effects of gas; it was fitted with two glass eye pieces, and a rubber valve through which the wearer exhaled.

4—M1914 equipment in a combination of leather and webbing. Originally intended for training only, it was issued in large numbers to the new volunteer battalions due to a shortage of webbing. It comprised a belt with a 'snake' clasp, shoulder braces, bayonet frog, entrenching tool helve attachment, tool head carrier, water bottle carrier, and two large pouches each holding 50 rounds—these last recalling the old Slade-Wallace equipment. (The leather water bottle cover illustrated is not a typical example—the cloth covering was officially retained.) Knapsack and haversack were of webbing with leather straps. Up to 1918 some units could still be seen wearing this equip-

ment in the trenches; where possible, webbing and leather sets were not mixed within one unit, but there were exceptions.

5—The mess tin, originally carried inside the haversack, now increasingly appeared slung outside it or on the knapsack in its drab cloth cover; the increased amounts of ammunition, grenades, and other items required in the trenches left no room for it. The D-section two-part mess tin changed little in basic design between the Napoleonic Wars and 1937.

6—M1902 service dress trousers.

7—Strictly non-regulation position for carrying the eating utensils ready to hand, seen in period photographs.

8—Khaki cloth puttees.

9—Hobnailed 'ammunition boots'.

10—SMLE rifle No.1 Mark III, .303in. calibre.

11—Breech cover, to protect the action of the rifle from wet and mud.

23

FRENCH INFANTRYMAN, VERDUN, 1916

The improvisations of autumn 1914, the terrible winter of 1914-15, and the partial and piecemeal appearance of new horizon blue uniforms in spring 1915 left the French infantry with a very motley appearance. During the second half of 1915 a degree of standardisation was achieved; from that point on the front line infantryman, dressed from head to foot in the new uniform, began to resemble the theoretical image foreseen in the regulations of 9 December 1914. One new and essential element was now added: the steel helmet. The French were the first to receive a general issue of helmets, which it was hoped would reduce the very high proportion of head wounds from bullets and shrapnel; it was supplied to front line troops from September 1915. The definitive outline of the 'Poilu' had now been achieved: the soldier who would be tested by fire and steel in the holocaust of Verdun.

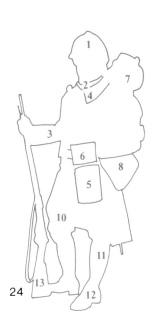

1—M1915 Adrian pattern steel helmet. Its supply was an impressive feat—more than three million were made and distributed before the end of 1915. Unfortunately, the protection it offered was inferior to that of the slightly later, and heavier, British and German models; the Adrian weighed only .765kg (1lb 11oz.) and was made of mild steel. Its complex shape was copied from that worn by contemporary firemen; it comprised a skull, a two-part brim and an applied raised crest, with a pressed metal badge on the front, this differing with arm of service. Issued with a blue-grey paint finish, it was provided from late 1915 with a more concealing fabric cover in light blue or khaki.

2—Blue cotton stock.

3—M1914/15 greatcoat. At the end of 1915, to allow the carrying of a further reserve of ammunition, a large reinforced pocket with a two-button flap was added to each side. This modification was made to already existing coat stocks, and there was often a contrast between the shades of cloth used; the illustrated coat is of a pale, imported fabric, but the added side pocket (just visible between gasmask and haversack) and the backing to various applied insignia are of standard horizon blue, noticeably darker.

4—The yellow arm-of-service collar patches briefly worn by infantry in the winter of 1914/15 were judged to be too visible; from May 1915 they were replaced by coat-colour patches with dark blue pipings and regimental numbers. This was also the colour selected for various rank and trade insignia worn on the uniform; our subject is a young corporal of the 7th Infantry, his rank marked by two short diagonal stripes on the forearms, and his one year of completed service by the small point-up chevron on his upper left sleeve—these 'sardines' were introduced in April 1916.

5—Canister, of iron painted grey-blue, for the TN model gasmask and its associated anti-gas goggles. This gasmask, in its canister of flattened oval section, was issued from the end of 1915.

6—Lebel rifle equipment. This had changed only in colour, brown leather being specified in the December 1914 regulations. The belt illustrated is of a simplified pattern with a single-prong buckle. The individual tool—here, M1915 wire cutters—is carried slung on the belt for ease of access.

7—Campaign pack. The simplified M1893/1914 knapsack of greenish grey canvas is stowed with spare boots, mess tin, tent accessories, the squad's folding canvas bucket, and a personally purchased type of groundsheet with one face lined with black rubberised material.

8—Beige cloth M1892 haversack.

9—M1877 two-litre water bottle covered in horizon blue cloth. This double-size water bottle was originally reserved for issue to troops in Africa, but it was extended to the whole army in summer 1915. The mug hangs from the cork-string of one of the double spouts.

10—M1914 *pantalon-culotte* trousers. Since April 1915 a yellow piping had been added to the outer seams—this is just visible in the rear view. Note the knee reinforcement patches provided for the harsh conditions of trench warfare.

11—Horizon blue cloth puttees.

12—M1912 boots modified 1916, with side reinforcement rivet.

13—M1907/15 rifle, popularly termed the Berthier, the first model with an angled bolt handle. Developed from the M1892 carbine, this was issued at the same time as the Lebel to make up required numbers. It was loaded with three-round charger clips of 8mm cartridges. The M1907 sling was made in brown leather from the end of 1914.

François Vauvillier

GERMAN INFANTRYMAN, VERDUN, FEBRUARY 1916

The regulations of 21 September 1915 standardised various modifications carried out since the beginning of the war—the blackening of leather equipment, etc.—and also introduced both a new greatcoat, and a new all-arms campaign tunic, the '*Bluse*'. Early in 1916 the useless *Pickelhaube* was replaced by an impressive and efficient steel helmet, first seen at Verdun. Now the German infantryman, too, had arrived at the appearance which would be characteristic of the latter half of the war, very different from the silhouette of 1914. This austere, drab outfit would hardly change before the Armistice. The only touch of colour was provided by the bayonet knot, in distinctive colours identifying the soldier's company. This grenadier of the 184th Infantry wears assault equipment, his knapsack laid aside for a lightened arrangement of immediately necessary items.

1—M1916 '*Stahlhelm*', hot-pressed from a hard silicon-nickel steel; more expensive than Allied helmets, which were cold-pressed, it was also heavier (2lb.10½oz./1.2kg), and gave better protection to face, ears and neck. It had an efficient internal sizing system of leather tabs and pads, and used the old M1891 chinstrap. Two external lugs allowed the fitting, at need, of an extra steel plate shaped to the front of the skull—the '*Stirnpanzer*'—for use by sentries and other particularly exposed personnel. Issued with a field grey paint finish, some helmets were later painted in an angular multi-coloured camouflage pattern of dull red/browns, ochres, greens and blue/greys divided by black lines. Various fabric covers were also used for extra concealment, the most common being of light khaki sandbag material.

2—M1914 tunic; our grenadier has not yet received the M1915 '*Bluse*'—in fact, all types of tunic including the M1907/10 were still to be seen in use right through the war. In regulation style this tunic lacks cuff patches and simulated skirt pocket flaps. The white piping of the shoulder straps was now common to all line infantry; note red '184' embroidered at the ends.

3—M1915 *Gummimaske*, now carried in a grey-painted metal canister which gave better protection than the old cloth bag, but which did not include a spare filter cartridge. The canister was carried on a sling; the mask could be arranged in the 'alert' position on the chest.

4—M1915 assault pack, consisting of the M1915 greatcoat rolled in the M1892 tent cloth, the ends strapped together, and the roll arranged round the M1910 mess tin—here a war-time example in enamelled metal painted field grey. The sling of the 'breadbag' and several straps allow the pack to be arranged and slung in this manner.

5—M1887 'breadbag', here an *ersatz* model in grey cloth, with only a single attachment loop on the flap.

6—M1907 water bottle, also of *ersatz* economy manufacture in sheet iron enamelled field grey, covered with coarse cloth of a neutral shade.

7—Individual tool, here the M1887 pick-hatchet in its black leather carrier.

8—Bayonet of wartime manufacture, its hilt and scabbard of steel painted field grey, secured to the tool helve in the usual way to stop it flapping and clattering when the soldier was on the move. The '*Troddel*' or bayonet knot was still of the traditional pre-war type, the various coloured sections identifying the company according to a complex sequence: this combination is that of the 10th Company.

9—M1895 belt; this, and one of the triple cartridge pouches, has been blackened as ordered in September 1915, the other has not—this kind of mixed equipment was not uncommon under front line conditions.

10—M1914 trousers in stone grey; wartime-made examples often lacked the regulation red seam piping.

11—M1866 boots in blackened leather.

12—M1898 Mauser rifle, 7.92mm calibre; this sling is of *ersatz* manufacture, of fabric with leather ends.

FRENCH ALPINE LIGHT INFANTRYMAN, 1916

A lone among the infantry, the battalions of Chasseurs—'light infantry'—were already entirely uniformed in a blue shade in August 1914, and needed less urgent reforms than the red-trousered 'lignards'. They were also very attached to their special uniform, which contributed to their threatening reputation among their opponents. Since the savage fighting in the Vosges mountains at the end of 1914 the Germans had christened them the 'Black Devils'—in Chasseur legend, edited to the more accurate 'Blue Devils'. The uniform they were wearing at the outbreak of war survived for a year and a half without major modification. The Chasseurs à Pied kept their uniform of képi, greatcoat and trousers entirely of blue, with yellow distinctives; and the Chasseurs Alpins—'alpine light infantry'— kept until early 1916 their special uniform of beret and tunic.

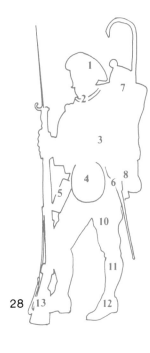

1—M1889 alpine beret, in very dark blue wool, with a bugle-horn badge cut out of yellow cloth on the right front.

2—Blue cotton stock

3—M1916 tunic, of the design termed 'vareuse-dolman', in 'blued-iron grey'. Hardly modified since its adoption in 1891, it had a very deep fall collar, two side pockets, and cuffs which could be folded down over the hands; it fastened with seven front buttons charged with a bugle-horn device. At the outbreak of war it had been worn in very dark blue, almost black, with simple yellow unit numbers on the collar. The colour changed to this dark blue-grey in 1915, and from 12 November that year the collar patches changed to this design—double pipings, a battalion number and a bugle-horn all in green on tunic colour. Until May 1916 the shoulders incorporated large pads at the outer end. The corporal illustrated wears the small rank stripes of the 1915 regulations, in the green of this arm of service; and has been awarded a Croix de Guerre.

4—M1915 Adrian helmet, painted blue-grey, and with the bugle-horn frontal badge of the Chasseur units.

5—Blue-grey painted iron canister, of rectangular section, for the M2 gasmask; it is suspended from one of the cartridge pouches. The M2, uniting goggles and a protective nose and mouth pad in one piece, was issued from spring 1916 until the beginning of 1918.

6—Brown leather Lebel rifle equipment. The Y-shape of the M1888/1914 bayonet frog allowed its use with the tunic tab which buttoned upwards between its branches and over the belt to help support the weight, a feature of French military jackets and coats since the later 19th century. The theoretical ammunition issue for line infantry was four packets of eight rounds in each of the front pouches, and three packets in the rear pouch, giving a total of 88 rounds. Shortly before the war the issue to Chasseurs was increased to 120 rounds.

7—Alpine type campaign pack, based on the M1893/1914 knapsack now in a new regulation pat-tern, in grey-green fabric and brown leather. There are two particular points of note: the curve-handled 'alpenstock' strapped to the left, and the cloak folded and stowed beneath the tent cloth at the top of the pack. This is the hooded M1892 'pélerine' of the alpine troops, fastened at the front by four small buttons; it was made in horizon blue from November 1915 onwards. The other elements of the pack are stan-dard: the M1852 mess tin, the individual tool (here the bill-hook), and an item of the squad's camping kit (here the large 'bouteillon' dixie, its name corrupted from that of its inventor Bouthéon).

8—Beige cloth M1892 haversack; this was seen in many different drab shades during the war.

9—M1877 two-litre water bottle covered in grey-blue cloth; slung on one of the cork-strings is the mug, here an example painted with a matt grey-blue varnish.

10—M1915 trousers in 'blued-iron grey', a shade slightly darker and bluer than the jacket, with yellow pipings. In August 1914 the Chasseurs wore straight trousers of the same colour, but since the beginning of 1915 they had received the new cut, tapered from the knee.

11—M1910 puttees in dark blue cloth; the Chas-seurs Alpins had been the first to receive puttees, in 1889, at which date they were considered 'athletic and hygienic'.

12—M1912/16 boots in blackened leather.

13—M1886/93 Lebel rifle, with its needle bayonet with cruciform section blade.

François Vauvillier

28

BRITISH INFANTRYMAN, SOMME OFFENSIVE, JULY 1916

The battle of the Somme, which opened on 1 July 1916 with a major British attack, in fact lasted until 19 November that year, in a series of operations which would cost the Allied and Axis armies about 600,000 casualties each. It is, however, the first day which has come to symbolise the sufferings of the 'Tommy' of the Great War. This was the first major offensive by Britain's 'New Army', largely composed of volunteers; their patriotic zeal was matched, to all appearances, by a plan and resources which justified great confidence. Instead, 1 July 1916 turned out to be the most costly single day in the British army's history: some 60,000 men were killed, wounded or made prisoner within a few hours, for minimal gains.

With regard to the appearance of the infantryman, two new elements are immediately noticeable: the steel 'shrapnel helmet', and the system of coloured unit emblems worn on the uniform. The soldier illustrated wears the battle insignia adopted by 'A' Company, 1st Battalion, Lancashire Fusiliers.

1—Mark I steel helmet, known as 'Brodie' after its inventor, manufactured from November 1915; by July 1916 a million had been delivered. The design gave protection from air-burst shrapnel and shell fragments, and allowed easy mass production using 'Hadfield's' manganese steel, with a weight of 2lb.2½oz. (.978kg). With the adoption of unit battle insignia on the uniform, badges and symbols were often painted on the helmet—here a representation of the yellow hackle traditionally worn in peacetime full dress headgear by the Lancashire Fusiliers.

2—M1902 SD tunic, as described on previous pages. The red cloth triangle sewn to each upper sleeve identified 29th Division, veterans of the Gallipolli campaign, who adopted it on arrival in France in March 1916. The units of the division also wore patches in traditional regimental colours on the back below the collar: quick unit identification in the attack was most important, and this position was clearest for following waves of troops. In the 1st Bn. Lancashire Fusiliers the red and yellow were arranged in geometric patches identifying the companies—a diamond, red left and yellow right, identified 'A' Company. (The need for quick identification had been recognised in the Boer War, when coloured flashes were sewn to helmet covers; the practice was reintroduced gradually and unevenly from mid-1915, but by no means all divisions had adopted systems of battle insignia by mid-1916.) The single chevron on each sleeve identifies a lance-corporal, the most junior non-commissioned rank. The vertical gold braid bar sewn to the left forearm is a wound stripe, as instituted in 1916. This regiment wore brass shoulder strap titles in the form of the fusiliers' traditional 'flaming grenade' over 'LF'.

3—M1908 webbing equipment, as described on previous pages. This is the arrangement known as 'fighting order', with the haversack worn on the back and containing mess tin, eating utensils, shaving kit, a groundsheet, and two days' rations of corned beef and biscuits. Note that the lower set of three cartridge pouches are of the modified pattern introduced from October 1914, with strap fasteners instead of simple press studs: when firing in the prone position or from trench parapets men reported that the original pattern easily came unfastened, with accidental loss of ammunition.

4—Extra ammunition bandolier, a simple cotton container with five pockets each holding two five-round clips.

5—Satchel for the 'PH' anti-gas hood.

6—General service shovel. By now it was clear that assault troops had to have tools which allowed quick repair and consolidation of enemy trenches, so that they could withstand the almost inevitable artillery fire and counter-attacks which the Germans were quick to unleash on any captured position. Picks, shovels, large wire cutters, empty sandbags, and even coils of barbed wire might add to the already heavy load of assault infantry.

7—M1902 SD trousers.

8—Khaki puttees.

9—Hobnailed 'ammunition boots'.

10—SMLE rifle No.1 Mark III*, a slightly simplified version of the Mark III introduced in 1916.

11—M1908/13 bayonet, fixed for the assault. The 1913 modification involved removal of the large quillon.

12—M1908 webbing rifle sling.

13—Wire cutters for attachment to the rifle, No.1 Mark II; they worked by pushing the rifle forward against a strand of wire caught between the cutter jaws.

ITALIAN ALPINE INFANTRYMAN, ITALIAN FRONT, 1916

Italy's northern frontiers lie through some of the most mountainous country in Europe; and in October 1872 the Kingdom of Italy ordered the raising of 15 experimental Alpine companies for defensive fighting in the high Alps. Raised by Gen.Perruchetti, these 'Alpini' wore a number of special uniform and equipment items compatible with their special rôle. In 1906 the Alpini were the first Italian troops to experiment with uniforms of neutral colour, to camouflage them in the grey, rocky terrain where they operated. The grey-green uniform was a success, and was extended to the whole army in 1909. Among Italy's best troops of the Great War, the Alpini made great sacrifices during the fighting in the eastern Alps against Austrian troops.

1—M1910 hat, modelled on a shape characteristic of the region in the 19th century, and adopted after an unsuccessful experiment with a 'melon'-shaped headgear. This felt hat, which proved very popular, is still in use today basically unchanged. The frontal badge, embroidered in black, shows a bugle-horn with the regimental number in the centre and crossed rifles, the whole surmounted by a spread eagle. On the left side was a pompon in battalion colour (white, red, green or blue respectively), and a black crow's-feather plume; this last was white for senior officers.

2—M1909 tunic, with standing collar and fly front. The collar patches (bearing the Savoy star common to all Italian soldiers) were in green for this arm of service. The cuffs are pointed; on each shoulder a roll of cloth helped prevent equipment straps from slipping. Regulation tunics had no exterior pockets, and the side pockets visible on this example are a personal addition of the owner. There were two short rear vents with single button fastening. A field dressing was carried in an interior pocket.

3—M1909 trousers, in the same grey-green as the tunic; these were of straight cut, gathered at the ankles by tapes, and had two oblique side pockets.

4—Woollen socks. These were at first issued only to mountain troops, but were later extended to all infantry fighting in mountain terrain.

5—M1909 puttees; like the woollen stockings, these were originally peculiar to mountain troops but were later issued much more widely.

6—M1912 ankle boots in brown leather, cut high at the ankle for support, and provided with climbing cleats. Again, this original Alpini issue item was extended to all infantry committed to the mountain front.

7—M1907 equipment; Italy was alone among the combatant nations in issuing leather harness coloured to match the uniform itself. It consisted of a belt with a single-prong buckle, a bayonet frog, a brace passing from the belt around the neck and back again, and two double cartridge pouches.

8—M1891 bayonet in leather scabbard.

9—M1907 haversack, accomodating rations and small personal effects.

10—M1907 water bottle, made of poplar or willow wood with iron strapping, and a leather tab by which it could be fixed to the belt or to the haversack.

11—M1916 'Polivalente Z' gasmask, carried in a green-painted metal canister; wood, or even cardboard were also used for this. A black-painted inscription read 'Anyone who loses his mask is risking death; keep it by you at all times'.

12—M1891 Mannlicher-Carcano rifle, 6.5mm calibre.

33

RUSSIAN INFANTRYMAN, EASTERN FRONT, WINTER 1916

For winter campaigning the Russian soldier was issued with the same basic uniform as for summer, but in a heavier woollen cloth. Over this was worn a heavy, generously cut greatcoat, and a fur or fleece cap; centuries-long experience of the rigours of extreme cold weather prompted various other improvised modifications. Nevertheless, the problems of supplying a huge army spread along a vast front were never solved with any consistency by the Imperial Russian command. The plight, and the morale, of the '*frontovik*' steadily declined under the terrible conditions, and the gulf between officers and men widened. This eventually led to the mutinies of 1917; to the replacement of the Imperial regime by the government led by Kerenski; and to the seizure of power by the Bolsheviks, who in March 1918 signed the Peace of Brest-Litovsk with the Germans, thus releasing large enemy forces to reinforce those on the Western Front—with severe consequences for the Western Allies.

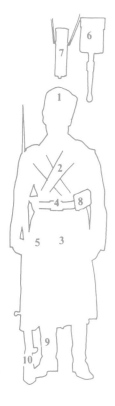

1—M1910 sheepskin cap, or '*papakha*', issued in either natural or artificial fleece of a drab grey-beige shade, with a greenish khaki cloth crown. The band could be turned down to protect neck and ears. The stamped metal cockade painted orange and black was pinned to the front of this cap, as on the visored summer cap.

2—The '*bashlyk*' was a traditional Russian item, best described as a hood with long tails, made in heavy beige wool. Its use was only officially allowed when the temperature sank to −5°C. It is worn here thrown back; when raised, the hood completely covered the head (including the headgear) and neck. Its tails are crossed at the front and tucked under the belt; when the hood was raised they were knotted.

3—M1881 greatcoat, still worn by many Russian troops despite the introduction of a new model from 1911. In fact it was superior for very cold weather, having a double-breasted front fastened by hooks, while the M1911 was single-breasted and had very visible brass buttons; and in 1917 the older style was officially reintroduced. Of grey-brown wool, it had a two-button integral half-belt at the rear, which was deeply pleated. The collar patches were in arm-of-service colours, here the raspberry red of the rifleman, as were the broad shoulder straps bearing a regimental monogram or number, e.g. a yellow '9' for the 9th European Rifles. This soldier's decoration is the St. George's Cross for enlisted ranks on its orange and black ribbon.

4—Riflemen wore blackened leather belts, here with the M1904 brass buckle plate stamped with the Imperial eagle.

5—'Stick' hand grenade.

6—'Linnemann' pattern entrenching tool in a cloth carrier. This was the most typical individual tool issued to Russian troops.

7—'Zelinski' pattern gasmask, carried in a narrow metal box painted green.

8—M1893 brown leather cartridge pouches, each holding six charger clips of five rounds; another 40 rounds were normally carried in the haversack.

9—Blackened leather boots of standard pattern. Shortages dictated the increasing issue of ankle boots and puttees in place of the traditional knee boots.

10—M1891 'three-line' Mosin Nagant rifle of 7.62mm calibre. The M1891 bayonet, always carried fixed, was unusual not only in having an archaic, musket-style socket fitting, but also in having the point flattened like a screwdriver.

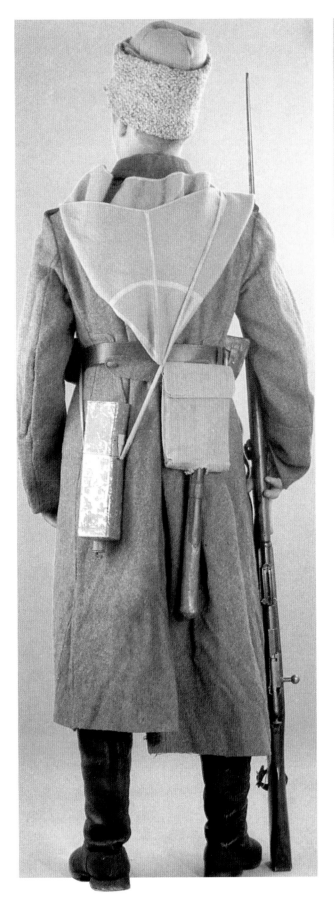 

FRENCH FOREIGN LEGIONNAIRE, WESTERN FRONT, 1916

From the first days of the war a constant stream of foreign volunteers allowed the creation of four 'march regiments' of the famous Foreign Legion, stiffened by veterans from North Africa. These units were dressed in the blue and red line infantry uniform, their allegiance to their famous corps being marked only by a few inconspicuous distinctions. In spring 1915, like the rest of the infantry, the Legion regiments received horizon blue uniforms. 1915 also saw a reduction in numbers, due both to very heavy battle casualties and to the detachment of several large contingents to serve with their national armies, Belgian, Italian and Russian.

In October 1915 the Legion units remaining on the Western Front were reorganised into a single 'march regiment' designated the RMLE. During the winter of 1915/16 their horizon blue uniforms were replaced by a mustard-khaki equivalent which was ordered for all units from the African garrison army. It was in this khaki that the RMLE covered itself with glory; it shared with the RICM ('*Régiment d'infanterie coloniale de Maroc*') the honour of being the most heavily decorated French regiment of the entire war.

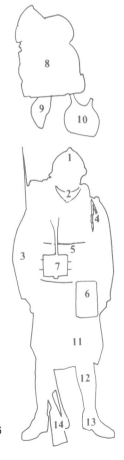

1—M1915 Adrian helmet; issued in grey-blue finish, this was repainted khaki in 1916 to match the rest of the new uniform. The Legion did not have a distinctive helmet badge, wearing the grenade and 'RF' motif of the infantry as a whole.

2—Khaki cotton stock.

3—M1915 greatcoat in mustard-khaki. In August 1915, after a crisis in uniform supply, the Ministry of War decided to stop production of the simplified M1914 coat and to reintroduce a double-breasted coat of classic cut. The large falling collar and the two cartridge pockets in the sides were retained; otherwise the coat returned to the M1877 design, with two rows of six front buttons, and false cuffs with a buttoned rear vent. This coat, also made in horizon blue, was issued to the African units in winter 1915/16. The only distinctives peculiar to the Legion were the collar patches bearing two pipings and the Legion's traditional grenade badge, in the green chosen as the Legion's distinctive colour under the 9 December 1914 regulations. Until the beginning of 1917 the patches were rectangular.

4—The collective citation lanyard or '*fourragère*', introduced in April 1916. For two or three citations in Army orders units received this in the green and red of the ribbon of the Croix de Guerre. The RMLE was thus honoured on 5 June 1916, and wore this lanyard for a year. Our légionnaire, a veteran of colonial campaigns, wears three individual medals: the Médaille Militaire, Croix de Guerre and Médaille Coloniale.

5—Blue woollen body-belt, 4.2m (more than 13ft.) long. This sash was typical of African units, providing warmth on cold desert nights and back support for heavily laden men on long marches. The Zouaves and Foreign Legion wore it in this colour; for parades it was worn visibly, over the coat and under the belt equipment.

6—Box for the M2 gasmask, here painted khaki.

7—Lebel rifle equipment in the new brown leather version: M1903/14 belt, M1892/1914 braces, and three M1916 pouches.

8—Campaign pack; this is the same as illustrated and described on pp.24-25, with the substitution of another item of squad camping equipment—the large '*bouteillon*' or dixie, here of a simplified wartime pattern without a handle on the cover, and with a non-reflective greyish finish.

9—M1892 haversack in light brown cloth.

10—M1877 two-litre water bottle with khaki cloth cover; by regulation the bottle was supposed to be slung with the smaller spout forward.

11—*Pantalon-culotte* trousers, M1914, of exactly the same pattern as the horizon blue trousers worn by the Metropolitan infantry. In theory all categories of infantry were supposed to have yellow seam piping, but under the conditions of wartime manufacture this was often omitted.

12—Khaki puttees. The mustard-khaki shade used for these uniforms was unstable, and one man might display a variety of tones in the different parts of his outfit. Generally the French-made fabric was of a yellower shade than the browner material imported from Britain.

13—M1912 boots, modified 1916.

14—M1907/15 rifle, calibre 8mm, known as the Berthier; here, the second pattern with a straight bolt handle. It is fitted with an M1915 bayonet, without quillon.

François Vauvillier

BELGIAN INFANTRYMAN, WESTERN FRONT, 1917

As illustrated and described on pp.4-5, the uniform and equipment issued to the Belgian infantryman at the outbreak of the Great War were completely unsuitable for the conditions of modern warfare. From the first battles of August 1914 it was clear that the archaic shako and ventral cartridge pouch needed replacement, and that the pack needed lightening. At the end of 1914 the infantry who fought on the Yser received a simplified outfit, but this was purely transitional while a completely new uniform and equipment were prepared.

In 1915 the new appearance of the Belgian infantryman was settled. It was clearly inspired partly by that of the French soldier, and both the helmet and the gasmask were supplied by France. The uniform was made of a khaki serge procured from Britain, however; and the equipment, very similar to the British M1908 pattern, was made in Britain by the Mills company. The Belgian infantryman thus presented a compromise between the outfits adopted by Belgium's two protecting allies.

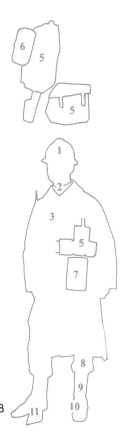

1—M1915 steel helmet, painted khaki; this was the Adrian, exactly as issued to French troops, apart from the frontal badge—the lion's mask emblem common to all branches of the Belgian army.

2—Cotton stock, khaki in colour, worn to protect the neck from the chafing of the standing collar of the tunic.

3–M1915 greatcoat, double-breasted and fastened by two rows of four buttons painted khaki and bearing a lion motif. It had two large side pockets with straight, single-button flaps. The large falling collar bore no insignia; the only distinctives displayed on campaign were the shoulder straps, piped in arm-of-service colours—here, the yellow of a Carabinier. There was an integral half-belt for rear waist adjustment, and below this two **vertical** pockets. Two buttons allowed the skirts **to be fastened up** for marching.

4—The coat hides an **M1915 tunic in** khaki serge, with a standing collar **rounded at the** front corners, which bore—for the **Carabiniers**—green collar patches piped in yellow. **The single-breasted** tunic had one row of buttons.

5—M1915 cotton webbing equipment, made in Britain by the Mills company. At first glance very similar to the British M1908 pattern, it in fact varied in many details. It consisted of two four-pocket cartridge pouch sets, arranged one-over-three on each side, each holding two five-round clips of 7.65mm ammunition, giving 80 rounds in all; shoulder braces with a hook-buckle system in front of the shoulder, engaging with the cartridge carriers and with both the top and bottom of a webbing knapsack—this latter with five sets of external stowage straps for the attachment of the tent cloth, blanket and mess tin. On the right of the belt was a webbing haversack; on the left, the bayonet frog, and a Linnemann entrenching tool reversed in a web carrier with the water bottle hanging over it, this latter of aluminium covered in khaki cloth and suspended in a web frame carrier. Like the British set, this equipment could be set up in various ways by means of the interchangeable strap and buckle fastenings; and could be put on or taken off in one piece, like a jacket, by fastening and unfastening the belt buckle only.

6—The mess tin was the same aluminium model as issued in 1914, but now painted in khaki.

7—French M2 gasmask, in its khaki-painted metal canister.

8—M1915 trousers in khaki serge; these were straight cut, with two slash side pockets, and an integral rear half-belt for adjustment.

9—Brown leather gaiters, identical apart from their colour to the old peacetime model; they laced up the front by means of hooks.

10—Standard ankle boots.

11—M1889 Mauser carbine, calibre 7.65mm.

ITALIAN INFANTRYMAN, ITALIAN FRONT, MARCH 1917

In this uniform the Italian army was committed to the Great War on the side of the Allies, rather than that of the Central Powers, largely due to a British diplomatic initiative. The 1882 Triple Alliance with Germany and Austria-Hungary had been prompted largely by colonial rivalry with France; and Austria-Hungary—Italy's former imperial ruler—could never be her natural ally, especially given Austro-Hungarian delay in meeting Italian demands over border territories. On 23 May 1915 Italy declared war on the Central Powers.

The M1909 grey-green uniform was of modern cut, and was retained with only minor changes to collar and pockets right up until the end of the Second World War. The appearance of the Italian infantryman would change little over the next two years, apart from the adoption of two items which modern conditions made vital to all the combatant armies: the steel helmet and the gasmask. It was in the outfit illustrated that the Italian infantryman went into the indecisive offensive of spring 1917 on the eastern front—the 'Tenth Battle of the Isonzo', whose title sums up the costly futility of these operations.

1—M1916 steel helmet. At first the Italian army had used the French Adrian design; this model was clearly derived from the Adrian, but was made in one piece. The branch of service and unit number were sometimes identified by a painted frontal badge. The factory finish was a dark grey-green.

2—Grey-green cloth helmet cover, worn to prevent reflection. A wide variety of covers were used, differing in material and small details. The badge was often embroidered or sewn to the front.

3—Metal eye-protectors, with a narrow horizontal aperture; these were intended to protect against small explosions and splinters.

4—M1909 grey-green tunic of standard design. The stand collar bore distinctive patches. In the line infantry these identified the brigade: the green and red example illustrated was worn by the Cremona Brigade, comprising the 21st and 22nd Infantry Regiments. Like all such patches it bears the star of Savoy.

5—M1907 leather equipment, as illustrated and described on pp.20 and 32.

6—M1907 ammunition pouches. Each of the two pockets in each double pouch held four charger clips each of six cartridges, giving the rifleman a basic load of 96 rounds.

7—The individual tool here is a hatchet carried in an M1891 holder, which also allows the attachment of the M1891 bayonet in its leather scabbard.

8—M1907 haversack, in canvas with leather straps; it had external loops allowing the attachment of various stowage, including the water bottle. This pack was the most important single item of the Italian soldier's campaign equipment, since it could be rigged either as a knapsack or as a slung haversack, and accomodated his rations and his small personal effects.

9—M1909 water bottle, of old-fashioned 'keg' design and made of poplar or willow wood; a leather attachment allowed it to be fixed either to the belt or to the haversack.

10—M1916 'Polivalente Z' gasmask, this example carried in a green-painted metal canister but often seen with a container of wood or cardboard. An inscription reminded the owner to keep it handy at all times, on pain of death.

11—M1909 trousers, straight-cut of the same grey-green cloth as the tunic, and tightened at the ankle with tapes. There were two slanted side pockets.

12—Woollen stockings were non-regulation, but from 1916 onwards they were tolerated.

13—M1909 puttees in grey-green cloth; originally limited to the *Alpini*, these were issued to the whole army when Italy entered the war.

14—M1912 brown leather ankle boots. Originally intended for the mountain troops, they were provided with heavy hobnails and cleats; when the bulk of the Italian infantry was committed to mountain fighting the boots were issued on a wider basis.

15—M1891 Mannlicher-Carcano rifle, 6.5mm calibre: the standard arm of the Italian army.

AUSTRIAN ASSAULT INFANTRYMAN, ITALIAN FRONT, 1917

From an early stage of the bloody confrontation which developed between Austro-Hungarian and Italian troops on the war's southern European front both sides formed assault units. The main lines of opposing trenches and mountain positions were more or less static as they were on the Western Front; and these assault troops were used to break the deadlock by mounting sudden raids, and to gather intelligence by daring reconnaissance missions. The Italian army named their shock troops 'Arditi'; the Austrians, 'Sturmtruppen'. Their success persuaded the Austrian high command to create larger assault detachments to serve side by side with conventional infantry formations. These units were given the most high-risk missions, and in major operations formed the spearhead of the infantry offensive, occupying the captured enemy front line trenches until they could be reinforced by larger formations. Due to the nature of their tasks and the extreme danger they faced, the Sturmtruppen adopted distinctive insignia based on the symbolism of the death's-head and the grenade — this being their favoured weapon.

1—M1916 Austrian steel helmet, very similar to the German pattern which inspired it but not identical - the fabric chinstrap, and the light brown paint scheme, distinguished it.

2—M1917 tunic in woollen cloth of the so-called 'nettle green' shade. This replaced the M1909 'pike grey' model, and, typically of wartime manufacture, was simplified in many details. It had a soft stand-and-fall collar, five unconcealed front buttons, and four front pockets with box pleats and three-point flaps. Many variations of cloth and colour are known, including field grey, a yellowish brown, and even 'grigio-verde' examples made from the huge quantities of uniform cloth captured from the Italians after the Austrian victory at Caporetto. This trooper wears on his collar the two six-point stars, made of bone or celluloid, which marked the rank of private first class.

3—M1915 gasmask, an Austrian version of the German army's 'Gummimaske'; the green-painted metal canister had a sling of light drab fabric.

4—Brown leather belt with a brass buckle plate bearing the Imperial Austro-Hungarian double-headed eagle device. As the war progressed an ersatz grey-painted iron plate became most common.

5—Double cartridge pouches in brown leather. Each of the four pouches held two five-round charger clips of 8mm ammunition, giving 40 rounds in all. Versions in various ersatz materials, such as canvas, are known.

6—'Head-breaker' trench club, a typical weapon for these raiding units who often fought hand-to-hand. A very wide variety of these improvised clubs were made, usually with a heavy lead-weighted head on a wooden handle.

7—Trench daggers were equally common among the Sturmtruppen. Again, there were many impro-

vised patterns, but this was the regulation issue, with a wooden grip and a double-edged blade, carried in a metal scabbard painted green or brown, and fixed to the belt by a leather or cloth tab.

8—'Tyrolian' rucksack-style pack, which gradually replaced the rigidly squared horsehide knapsack from 1916 onwards. Practical, comfortable, and with a large and flexible carrying capacity, it was made in strong green or brown canvas. The broad straps had front braces which hooked to rings on the rear face of the ammunition pouches, helping to distribute the weight of the pack.

9—The Austrian version of the German army's 'breadbag', in green or brown canvas. This could be slung round the body or attached to the belt with loops and hooks. The interior was divided into compartments to take the water bottle, the mess tin, and rations.

10—Trench periscope: a simple metal tube with internal mirrors, painted matt green.

11—Water bottle in enamelled metal, painted green. Although normally carried inside the haversack, it had various suspension fittings allowing it to be carried externally.

12—M1917 trousers in nettle green; these had two tightening buttons below the knee. They were later replaced by mountain troops' semi-breeches.

13—Puttees; these were made of many varieties and shades of cloth.

14—Standard issue brown leather ankle boots.

15—M1895 Steyr-Mannlicher rifle, 8mm calibre, with M1895 bayonet.

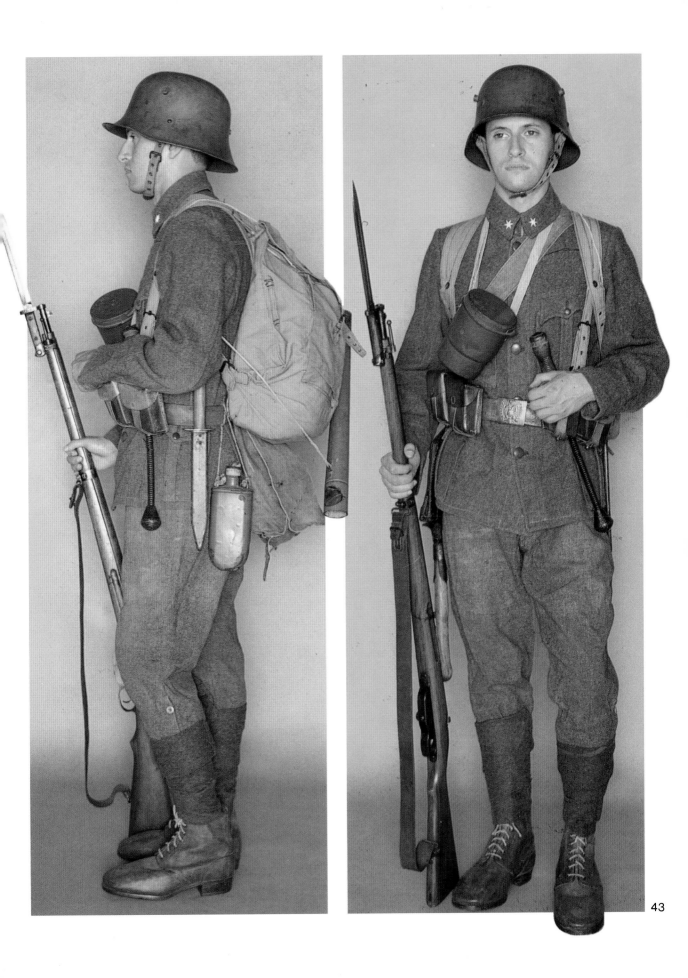

43

ITALIAN ASSAULT INFANTRYMAN, ITALIAN FRONT, 1917

From the beginning of the war on this southern European front the difficulties of the mountain terrain, and the solid nature of the Austro-Hungarian defensive lines, imposed special problems on the Italian army. Especially in the north-western sector, the prospect of mounting major offensives was daunting: the difficulty of assembling and moving up men and large amounts of matériel, and the exposure of all but stealthy movements to enemy artillery observers on higher ground, more or less confined offensive tactics to small-scale raids and scouting missions. Consequently, special assault sections were formed to carry out these 'commando'-style tasks; and in time formed units were incorporated within infantry battalions. These '*Arditi*' ('bold ones') also had a mission in conventional offensive operations, when they were committed to seizing key enemy positions to clear the way for their comrades. In 1917 these sections were reorganised by one Captain Barri, receiving uniform and equipment items adapted for their kind of mission. These forerunners in the most modern assault tactics faced extraordinary hazards, and earned a reputation unique in the Italian army.

1—M1916 helmet. After various unsatisfactory experiments Italy adopted this design based on the French Adrian, but pressed from a single piece of steel. It was issued in a grey-green painted finish, with the branch-of-service badge and regimental number stencilled on the front. As in the other combatant armies, helmets were soon generally worn with anti-reflective cloth covers of drab shades, which varied in exact colour depending upon material, age and weathering.

2—M1909 tunic in grey-green cloth, of a design similar to that issued to the *Bersaglieri* cycle troops. It had an open collar, here bearing patches in the black colour distinctive to the *Carbonari* of the Venetian Republic, upon whom the *Arditi* chose to model their traditions. Breast pockets were made both with and without pleats, and with single-button flaps. A large 'poacher's' pocket was provided at the back, to hold Thévenot explosive charges. Three large front buttons were concealed by a fly; and there were two buttoned belt loops. On the left sleeve can be seen the arm-of-service badge, a sword wreathed with laurel or oak, embroidered in black on a grey-green backing.

3—Regulation issue woollen sweater, grey-green in colour and with a roll neck; it was modelled on a type issued to the *Alpini*.

4—M1909 trousers, similar to those worn by the *Alpini* but more generously cut in the thigh to give greater ease of movement.

5—Woollen stockings; again borrowed from the mountain troops' uniform, these were considered more practical than puttees.

6—M1912 brown leather ankle boots, high in the ankle and fitted with climbing nails and cleats.

7—M1907 leather equipment. This was reduced to the minimum for the *Arditi's* special missions: the belt and a single ammunition pouch, the weight being sufficiently supported by the tunic belt loops.

8—The all-purpose M1907 haversack, used in the assault to carry quantities of hand grenades.

9—M1916 'Polivalente Z' gasmask in its painted metal container.

10—Water bottle, of the model which replaced the old wooden type; of a more conventional, flattened silhouette, it was made of aluminium covered with grey-green cloth, and looped to the belt by a strap. Among the *Arditi* it was traditional to carry brandy as often as water.

11—Fighting knife, here the regulation issue, although improvised knives and clubs for hand-to-hand fighting were often seen among these raiders. This type was made from an M1870 Vetterli bayonet, with wooden grips, and a blackened leather Vetterli scabbard.

45

FRENCH INFANTRYMAN IN ASSAULT EQUIPMENT, SUMMER 1917

The reform of French uniforms achieved under the difficult conditions of 1914 and 1915 had monopolised the efforts of the authorities, and no comparable reform of personal equipment had taken place. Sadly, an improvement which had in fact been approved in 1913—-the replacement of the slings of the haversack and water bottle by attachments fixing them directly below the belt kit—had been 'forgotten' in the turmoil. All in all, the regulation equipment of the French infantryman remained throughout the war more or less unchanged from that worn at the end of the previous century.

If it was cumbrous and uncomfortable on the march, the full knapsack equipment was simply impossible for troops going into the assault over the shell-churned moonscape of the Western Front. Consequently the high command eventually authorised a lightened 'assault order' for men in the leading waves.

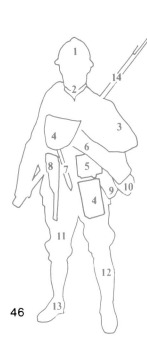

1—M1915 Adrian pattern steel helmet. Interestingly, from summer 1916 onwards the cloth helmet covers were ordered abandoned on the grounds that scraps of cloth—which were naturally filthy, due to trench conditions—were being carried into head wounds with serious medical consequences. Stocks of absolutely matt grey-blue paint were issued instead, and new helmets were finished in this way at the factories. Our assault trooper has adopted a solution occasionally, if rarely seen in the French army: splashes of brown, green and ochre paint over the grey-blue base in an attempt at camouflage.

2—Blue cotton stock.

3—M1914/15 tunic. Although issued to each soldier, this was seen usually as a barracks and walking-out garment behind the lines; the greatcoat was the 'principal battle garment', and the tunic was only worn under it in very cold weather. On rare occasions, however, the tunic was worn alone during summer operations. The tunic had a standing collar, and fastened by a hook-and-eye and five small uniform buttons; cuffs and shoulders were quite plain. There were two side pockets, and on the left side only a buttoning belt loop. The collar patches bear the cypher and pipings of the 51st Infantry Regiment; the additional coloured disc, introduced in July 1916, identified the battalion—here, yellow for the 3rd Battalion. On the left upper sleeve are three service chevrons (the first for 12 months' service, and another for each six months' service thereafter), above a flaming grenade badge marking this man's combat speciality. The large white patch sewn to the back helped commanders to keep track of the progress of the assault through their binoculars.

4—M2 gasmask in 'alert' position; its canister hangs in the usual position below the left hand pouch.

5—The usual Lebel rifle equipment in brown leather, here with the simplified single-prong buckle.

6—Assault pack. The knapsack was left in the jumping-off trench, and a horseshoe roll was made up with the blanket and tent section. The tent pegs and cords were not carried; they were useless in the fighting line, where the tent section was used as an all-purpose groundsheet or shelter-half. The roll was strapped together at the ends; another strap often secured a bundle of empty sandbags, to be filled at need, e.g. to help fortify a shellhole if the squad was pinned down.

7—Fighting knife, here the M1915 made by cutting down an M1886 bayonet and fitting it with a wooden grip and leather scabbard.

8—Individual tools were slung from the belt; here, the M1909 Seurre pattern pick-spade. Other troops might carry M1916 general service picks and shovels with removable helves shortened for ease of carrying.

9—Two M1892 haversacks; one contained rations, the other grenades and signalling equipment. An OF1916 grenade is also carried clipped to the belt.

10—Two two-litre water bottles; the difficulty of supplying clean water to men in close combat was considerable, and had prompted the introduction of the double-sized water bottle in 1915. In the assault one bottle typically contained wine mixed with water, the other coffee and *tafia* spirit.

11—M1914 trousers in horizon blue (note different shades of different parts of the uniform) with yellow seam piping.

12—Puttees in light grey-blue cloth.

13—M1912 boots, modified 1916.

14—M1907/15 'Berthier' rifle, carried slung by this grenadier.

François Vauvillier

46

RUSSIAN INFANTRYMAN, EXPEDITIONARY CORPS, FRANCE, 1917

To provide a visible demonstration of inter-Allied solidarity Tsar Nicholas II agreed, at the urging of President Poincaré, to send an expeditionary corps of Russian troops to fight on the Western Front. The men who made up these two brigades of two regiments each were handpicked; all could read and write (!), and met the recruiting standards then in force for the Imperial Guard. All the officers were fluent in French. The uniforms and insignia were Russian, but the equipment and weapons were provided by the French army in order to avoid re-supply problems, particularly of ammunition. The Russian Expeditionary Corps was commanded first by General Palitzine, and subsequently by General Zankeleievitch; it conducted itself well under fire, until the news of events in Russia in 1917 — and the murderous losses sustained during the Nivelle offensive—sapped its morale. The corps was withdrawn from the Western Front in 1918.

1—M1915 Adrian helmet supplied by France; Russia did not manufacture a national pattern of helmet during the war. The two million examples provided to Russia were distinguished by a double-headed eagle badge on the front, and were painted khaki. The helmet was issued to the Russian expeditionary corps in France and in Macedonia.

2—'*Gymnastiorka*' shirt-tunic M1912 in summer weight cotton, the standing collar fastened (here, at the front) by two small buttons. This pullover garment had a buttoned vent to mid-chest. The examples issued to the expeditionary corps were made both in Russia and in France. The only insignia were the large, stiff shoulder boards, which for the expeditionary corps were khaki, sometimes piped with white. The chest badge worn here is that of a 3rd class marksman; note how it is attached to the leather brace.

3—Russian M1914 belt in brown leather, much narrower than the old type with a buckle plate, and fastened by a single-prong buckle.

4—French M1892/1914 shoulder braces in brown leather, a Y-strap arrangement which hooked to rings mounted on the rear of each of the cartridge pouches.

5—French M1905/14 (or M1916) ammunition pouches in brown leather; the front pair each held 10 charger-clips of three 8mm cartridges, the rear one eight clips, giving a total of 84 rounds for men armed with the M1907/15 'Berthier' rifle.

6—French M1892 haversack, containing rations.

7—French M1877 two-litre water bottle in tinned iron, covered with old horizon blue uniform cloth, with the usual '*quart*' or mug slung from one of the cork-strings.

8—Russian M1910 haversack, made of a proofed grey-beige canvas and with leather flap straps. This contained changes of clothing and reserves of ammunition. Its long, wide sling could be fixed in different ways, including an arrangement which allowed it to be worn on the back like a knapsack.

9—French M2 gasmask in its blue-painted metal canister; some were painted khaki to match the uniform.

10—M1907 semi-breeches, in cotton or wool depending on the season. Loose in the thigh, they tapered to the knee in order to tuck easily into the boots. There were two slash side pockets. Like all the uniform items issued to the expeditionary corps they might be made in Russia, in France of French material, or in France of Russian material—the latter, in the case of those illustrated.

11—Traditional blackened leather knee boots.

12—M1907/15 'Berthier' rifle, 8mm calibre, as issued to all personnel of the two brigades apart from the machine gunners, whose personal weapon was the M1892 carbine.

13—French M1915 bayonet, without quillon.

UNITED STATES INFANTRYMAN, ST.NAZAIRE, JUNE 1917

The entry into the war of the United States in 1917 was the decisive event which made final Allied victory certain. The USA's vast population and vibrant industrial base allowed her to transform her small peacetime army of 200,000 men into a force of more than three million in record time. The strong expeditionary force which the USA sent to France added decisively to the Allies' resources in the last phase of a war which had already dragged on for three years.   The first 'doughboys' to come ashore at St.Nazaire in June 1917 made an immediate impression, as much by their fitness and enthusiasm as by their well-made, modern uniforms and equipment. Profiting by their experience in the Spanish-American War at the turn of the century, the USA had put their whole army into khaki from 1902 onwards; and their equipment was in the canvas duck and cotton webbing introduced by Capt.Anson Mills in his experiments of 30 years before. This soldier of the 28th Infantry Regiment, 1st Division wears the complete marching equipment as he disembarks with the first contingents of the American Expeditionary Force.

1—M1912 campaign hat in khaki-brown rabbitskin felt, its peak shaped in the 'Montana' style and pierced by four ventilation eyelets. There was a leather sweatband inside, and a practical leather chinstrap; the cords, ending in a slider and 'acorns' at the front, were in arm-of-service colours for the enlisted ranks: pale blue for the infantry.

2—M1912 khaki tunic—in American usage, 'olive drab'—with a stand collar and four patch pockets with single-point flaps. The five large front buttons and four small pocket buttons bore the American eagle device. Dulled bronze collar discs bore the 'US' cypher on the right side; and the emblem of the branch of service on the left—here, the crossed rifles of the infantry—with the regimental number above and the company letter below.

3—M1912 semi-breeches, tapered to fit into the leggings and reinforced at the knees. These had two slanting front hip pockets, two rear hip pockets, and a right front fob pocket. Infantrymen received them with loops at the waist for a fabric belt.

4—M1910 rifle belt ('dismounted cartridge belt'); each of the ten pouches held two five-round charger clips, giving a total of 100 rounds. The pouches fastened with press studs bearing the American eagle.

5—M1910 first aid pouch, fastened by two plain press studs, and containing a field dressing in a sealed metal box.

6—M1910 water bottle ('canteen') with its cup, into which the bottom of the canteen fitted; the whole assembly fitted into a fabric carrier lined with felt for coolness, and closed by two tabs with press studs.

7—M1910 haversack (top) and pack carrier (below), the combination worn for the march. The haversack, with two front suspender/belt attachments and one rear, contained rations, washing kit, and (in the detachable flap pouch) the mess tin. The M1905 Springfield bayonet attached to the left in its M1910 fabric and leather scabbard; and the M1910 shovel in its carrier to the rear, under the 'meat can pouch'. The awkwardly long pack carrier accomodated changes of clothing, the blankets, groundsheet/poncho, tent cloth and accessories. The disadvantages of this pack, which was modern and scientific for its day, were that it was complicated to assemble; could not be worn without the belt, since it had suspenders but not shoulder straps; and—worst of all—would only accomodate the official load, and no extra front line necessities.

8—M1910 canvas leggings, laced through eyelets at the front.

9—M1904 'marching shoes' in russet brown leather, flesh side in and 'rough' side out; comfortable for dry weather, they were inadequate in the sodden trenches of France.

10—Springfield M1903/05 rifle in calibre .30-06, with M1907 sling. This excellent bolt-action rifle, generally based on the Mauser, served on well into World War II.

51

GERMAN INFANTRYMAN, ASSAULT BATTALION, WESTERN FRONT, 1918

Like the Italians and the Austrians, the German army formed specialist assault units for raiding and for spearheading attacks. The 'Sturm' Battalions, organised within each Army for operations on its sector of the front, contained not only infantrymen but many specialists: assault gunners with light cannon, machine gunners, trench mortar crews, and engineers with flame-throwers. The men carried large 'general service' tools rather than merely entrenching tools, enabling them to dig in quickly and consolidate captured positions while awaiting reinforcement by the conventional infantry. The favoured weapons included hand-to-hand daggers, clubs and entrenching spades sharpened into hatchets, and — in particular—large numbers of grenades. The formation of this type of unit marked a radical change in tactics—a concentration on exactly-timed, small-scale shock assaults on specific targets rather than the large frontal assaults which had invited such murderous losses. The war was truly becoming a matter for professionals.

1—M1918 steel helmet, differing from the M1916 by the substitution of a new, improved chinstrap and attachments. In the last weeks of the war a parallel type appeared, with cut-outs in the lower edges at each side to reduce the 'echo chamber' effect of the bell-shaped skull.

2—M1915 'Bluse', the new tunic intended to replace the M1907/10 and M1914 (although both continued to be seen alongside it). The Bluse was made in dark field grey cloth with a fall collar faced with green. The six large front buttons were concealed by a fly; and it had two slanted, flapped side pockets. The shoulder straps were narrower, and detachable; nevertheless they were often sewn firmly down to the shoulders, to prevent snagging. They were piped, in white for infantry, and bore the regimental number or monogram in red. The 1915 tunic was of the same design for the whole army, though made in a greener shade for the Light Infantry and Rifles units (Jäger and Schützen).

3—Patronen-Tragegurte, a supplementary cartridge bandolier in drab light grey cloth, its ten pockets holding a total of 14 five-round clips (70 rounds).

4—Two sandbags slung like 'waterwings', holding supplies of hand grenades ready to hand; these were popular among assault troops.

5—M1895 belt in blackened leather, here with an M1915 grey-painted Prussian belt plate.

6—M1915 'stick' grenade.

7—M1822 'general service' spade, carried in a cloth case reinforced with leather; this was attached at the left rear of the belt, the helve being secured to the tunic shoulder strap by a short strap or thong. These full-size tools allowed shock units to dig in rapidly, installing their machine guns and trench mortars in newly captured positions.

8—M1917 Lederschutzmaske gasmask, in waterproof leather with a filter cartridge. Its grey-painted metal canister was slung on a fabric strap.

9—Trench dagger, as carried by most assault troops, who often fought hand-to-hand.

10—Grey cloth bag looped to the belt, holding a spare filter cartridge for the M1915 gasmask.

11—Mauser Kar98A carbine, 7.92mm calibre, as issued to the assault units; it was carried slung, to leave the hands free.

12—M1917 trousers in field grey cloth, reintroducing this colour which had been abandoned in 1914. By this stage of the war the cloth was eaked out with ersatz fibres for economic reasons—even nettle fibres were used—and was of poor quality. The Sturmtruppen also used stocks of the mountain troops' special trousers; and elbows and knees were often reinforced with leather patches.

13—Puttees, now made out of any available cloth, German or Allied, of a wide range of drab shades.

14—M1901 ankle boots in brown leather, laced up with eyelets and hooks.

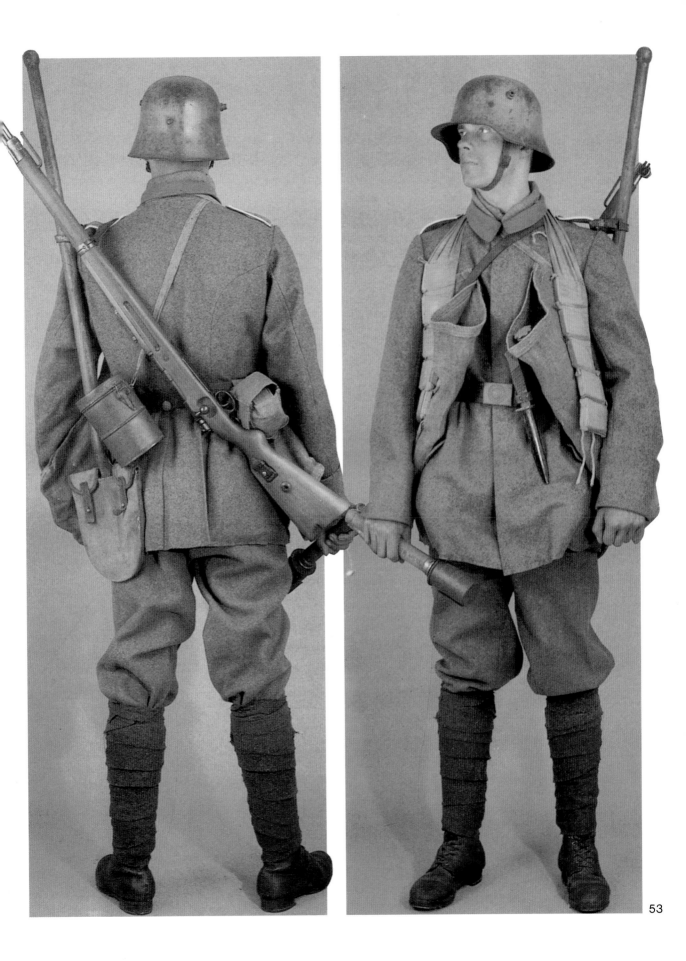

53

US INFANTRYMAN, WESTERN FRONT, SUMMER 1918

After a period of training in French rear areas the 'doughboys' (or 'Sammies', as the French and Germans called them) discovered the realities of trench warfare which had so worn down the armies of their allies and enemies. They quickly acquired and adapted those necessary items which had not been provided by the US Army. At first the steel helmet and gasmask ('small box respirator') were supplied by the British, but subsequently they were manufactured in America. Various other items were also supplied at this time, such as tools of different kinds, and trench knives. After some months of combat the adoption of puttees, and of more solidly made boots, became widespread. The American infantryman now looked very like his British comrades; but he was still distinguished by a fresh, aggressive air, which would not be found wanting when it was tested to the limit in the great German offensive of 1918.

1—M1917 steel helmet, copied from the British M1916 which had been supplied initially to the American Expeditionary Force. It was made of manganese steel and painted non-reflective khaki brown with a 'sanded' finish. The internal lining system was in black proofed material and the chinstrap in brown leather. In the last months of the war the AEF following the British example and began painting divisional insignia on the front of the helmet.

2—M1918 tunic in olive drab wool. This was simplified by the placing of pockets internally, only the flaps remaining visible. Each of the chevrons on the left forearm indicated six months' overseas service.

3—M1917 gasmask, copied from the British 'small box respirator', comprising a heavy face mask of rubberised cloth with an 'accordion'-style tube connecting it to a filter cartridge carried permanently in the haversack, slung on the chest here in the battle position.

4—M1917 cartridge belt, its ten pouches containing a total of 100 rounds. They were fastened by an improved press stud system, the so-called 'lift-the-dot' type.

5—M1917 trench knife, with a wooden grip, a guard in the form of a set of 'knuckle-dusters', and a strong triangular-section blade. Like many items of equipment, it was attached to eyelets along the bottom of the belt by patent brass hooks.

6—M1910 canteen and cup assembly, carried in a felt-lined fabric pouch fastened by two tabs and press studs.

7—Supplementary cartridge bandolier in light khaki cotton, slung by means of a tape of the same material which was simply adjusted by knotting. Each of the five pouches held two five-round charger clips of .30-06 ammunition. Again copied directly from the British equivalent, these bandoliers were issued fully loaded.

8—M1912 olive drab semi-breeches, tapered to the knees and calves. These trousers remained unchanged during the war.

9—Puttees in an olive drab shade close to that of the uniform. They were rapidly adopted after the AEF had a taste of trench warfare; the laced canvas leggings, which looked neat and strong, were in fact too complex and fragile for the rigours of the front line, and were quickly abandoned.

10—M1917 boots, in heavy brown hide; these were much more serviceable than the M1904 'russet marching shoes' which they replaced, and which had proved inadequate protection against the constant wet of the trenches. The M1904 pattern were relegated to use for walking-out and parades behind the lines.

11—M1903/05 Springfield rifle, .30-06 calibre, and leather M1907 sling.

BRITISH LIGHT MACHINE GUNNER, WESTERN FRONT, 1918

A steady increase in infantry firepower had brought to the infantry platoon its own automatic support weapon; by 1916 all British battalions had 16 Lewis light machine guns. The Lewis gunners wore a lightened set of equipment, since they did not carry rifles.

The overall appearance of the British 'Tommy' in the desperate defensive battles of spring 1918 which stopped the German 'Michael Offensive', and in the final breakthrough and advance of summer and autumn which forced Germany to the negotiating table, had changed much less than that of his French and German counterparts—testimony to the generally sound design of the kit with which he went to war.

1—Mark I steel helmet of the second pattern, with a turned steel rim instead of a raw edge. The non-reflective paint used for helmets varied in colour; the earlier helmets were generally finished in a drab greenish colour, the later ones in a yellower brown shade.

2—M1902 service dress tunic. The last year of the war saw the very widespread use of divisional insignia sewn to both upper sleeves; in this case it is the red and green rose of the 55th (West Lancashire) Division, a first class Territorial formation which had been in France since January 1916, and which distinguished itself in a stubborn stand at Givenchy-Festubert in April 1918. Brigade and battalion within the division were identified by systems of coloured geometric patches worn on the back below the collar, and thus hidden here. On the left forearm an embroidered khaki badge, 'LG' and a wreath, identifies a qualified Lewis gunner.

3—Leather jerkin, adopted from the winter of 1914/15 onwards and almost universally worn in bad weather thereafter. It was made of leather of differing shades of brown, usually in four large panels but sometimes of 'off-cuts', giving a 'patchwork' effect. Lined with khaki woollen material, or sometimes with fleece, it was strong, comfortable and popular. The classic pattern is illustrated, made of four panels of a russet brown shade, and fastened by four large leather-covered front buttons.

4—Light personal equipment, here based on the M1914 leather set described in its classic pattern on p.22. Instead of the rifle ammunition pouches this light machine gunner has an open-topped holster, simply closed with a strap, and an ammunition pouch for his personal defensive weapon. The revolver holster and 12-round pouch could also be attached to the M1908 webbing equipment belt and braces; they were regulation issue for appropriate troops from 1914. The belt, braces, entrenching tool, haversack and canteen carrier are as on p.23; again, note that the leather covering of the canteen is non-standard.

5—Webley Mark VI revolver, .455in. calibre; while other types were issued, this was the regulation sidearm from 1915 for officers and for specialist troops who did not carry rifles. The big pistol is secured by a khaki neck lanyard engaging with the butt ring of the revolver.

6—M1917 'small box respirator'. The definitive British gasmask, this much superior design remained in use almost until the end of World War II. A face mask of strong rubberised cloth with two glass eye pieces was connected by an 'accordion'-type tube of cloth-covered rubber to a metal filter cartridge; this remained permanently in the canvas haversack provided, whose adjustable fabric sling allowed it to be carried on the chest in action. The haversack was slung round the body when out of action, or on top of the knapsack on the march.

7—M1902 service dress trousers.

8—Khaki serge puttees.

9—'Ammunition boots'. In 1918 there was some limited issue of a second pattern with reinforced toes and heels.

10—Lewis light machine gun, .303in. calibre. This air-cooled weapon was the standard light automatic of the last three years of the war. The barrel was surrounded by a large cooling sleeve. It was fed by 47-round drum magazines, carried either in special round webbing pouches replacing the normal cartridge carriers or in canvas bucket-style bags by other members of the section. (At more than 30lb., 15kg, the gun itself was enough of a load for the gunner.) Its rate of fire, at 550 rounds per minute, was a welcome support for the rifle sections of the platoon; unfortunately it was also prone to jamming.

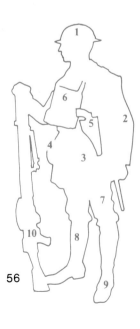

US INFANTRYMAN, FRENCH 157TH DIVISION, FRANCE, JULY 1918

The question of including black troops in the American Expeditionary Force caused the US Government some embarrassment in an age of racial segregation and unthinking prejudice. In the event the US 92nd Division was formed from regiments of black infantrymen; and later contingents arrived in France to form the 93rd Division, at least on paper. In fact the four regiments intended for this formation—the 369th, 370th, 371st and 372nd Infantry—were transferred to the command of the French army, forming the infantry of the French 157th Division 'Goybet'. The enlisted men and many officers of this division were black; the French, long used to a multi-racial colonial army, were less sensitive in these matters, and appreciated this useful reinforcement. For practical reasons the division was entirely equipped from French stocks, though retaining American uniforms.

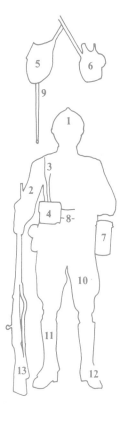

1—M1915 Adrian helmet painted dull blue-grey, with a narrow brown leather chinstrap. The frontal badge of the French Metropolitan infantry, a flaming bomb or 'grenade' with the cypher 'RF' (for *République Française*), is worn in all known photographs of the 157th Division; a special helmet with an American front badge exists, but it is not thought to have been distributed.

2—M1917 US Army olive drab tunic, slightly simplified from the M1912 design but still with the four full patch pockets; examples tend towards a browner shade of drab. The collar discs bore 'US' (right) and on the left the number of the regiment.

3—M1892/1914 equipment braces in brown leather; each of the three branches of the 'Y' was fitted with a detachable metal hook which engaged with a ring on the upper rear of one of the cartridge pouches.

4—M1916 French cartridge pouches in brown leather. Their external shape had not changed since 1888, but the method of attachment, modified in 1905, reached its final form in 1916.

5—French M1892 haversack in light brown cloth, containing the daily rations and small personal effects.

6—M1877 French two-litre water bottle in enamelled metal covered with old horizon blue uniform cloth. The enamelled iron mug was normally carried slung by its handle on one of the water bottle's cork strings.

7—French ARS type gasmask, the last model issued during the Great War, which appeared from November 1917. The fluted metal canister was painted khaki.

8—M1903/14 brown leather belt, with plain two-prong buckle.

9—M1915 bayonet, slung in its metal scabbard on the left side of the belt in (obscured here) a brown leather Y-shaped M1888/1914 frog.

10—M1912 US Army semi-breeches in olive drab, amply cut in the thigh and tapered from the knee down. These had five pockets: two oblique front hip, two rear hip, and a right fob pocket. Loops round the waist band allowed their use with a fabric belt when in shirtsleeve order.

11—US Army M1917 canvas webbing leggings, distinguishable from the earlier model by the side lacing and increased number of hooks and eyelets. In the black units both types of leggings and puttees were often seen worn together within any one unit.

12—M1917 brown leather boots, flesh side out, with double sewn soles often reinforced with nails.

13—French M1907/15 'Berthier' rifle, 8mm calibre, with M1907/14 brown leather sling.

59

FRENCH LIGHT MACHINE GUNNER, WESTERN FRONT, SUMMER 1918

The French army, like the British, recognised the importance of giving small infantry units their own automatic support weapon from 1915 onwards. (For the Germans, normally on the defensive in strong fixed positions, the heavy traverse-mounted machine gun was more consistently suitable, and it was not until 1918 that they issued a lighter and more portable version.) The French solution to the problem was the '*fusil-mitrailleur M1915 CSRG*', the acronym standing for the inventors and manufacturers, Chauchat-Sutter-Ribeyrolles-Gladiator. It was universally known as the 'Chauchat'; a mediocre weapon much prone to stoppages, it was still better than nothing at a time when infantry committed to major offensives desperately needed a better means of delivering firepower than bolt-action rifles. The team normally consisted of two men, a gunner and an ammunition carrier, who were burdened by an enormous weight of ammunition (36kg, nearly 80lb.) in addition to the 9kg (nearly 20lb.) of the gun itself, and their personal equipment. By spring 1918 the team had been increased to four, with this load more sensibly distributed between them. By that date each company had 12 Chauchat teams.

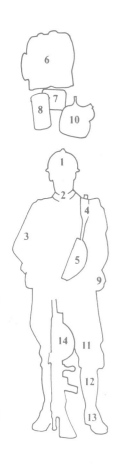

1—M1915 Adrian helmet, painted blue-grey.

2—Blue cotton stock.

3—M1915 greatcoat in horizon blue; this model, which reverted to the traditional cut with two rows of six buttons, was distributed to Metropolitan infantry only during 1917 after the exhaustion of stocks of the simplified M1914/15. Here it bears the collar patches of the 122nd Infantry Regiment, in the new lozenge shape ordered in January 1917, surmounted by the red disc indicating the 2nd Battalion. The four chevrons on the upper left sleeve mark two and a half years' service. Below them is the insignia of a qualified light machine gunner. This man has been awarded the Croix de Guerre, its bronze star indicating a citation in regimental orders.

4—M1892/1914 equipment suspenders and M1903/14 belt in brown leather. The special equipment for machine gun teams was compatible with these standard items.

5—M1916/17 magazine pouches, semi-circular in shape, each holding two magazines. Initially the curved side was worn inwards; but in May 1917 this revised layout was adopted, with a strap around the man's back to prevent them sliding together at the front under the weight of the magazines.

6—M1917 special knapsack for LMG teams. Outwardly similar to the standard M1893, it had an internal metal frame to support the weight of 12 more magazines. Note the quick-release fastening on the right shoulder strap, allowing the gunner to drop his pack quickly and arrange his ammunition reserve close at hand when firing prone. The external stowage includes the tent and blanket roll, the mess tin, and —here—a billhook: in theory the heavily burdened gunner was not supposed to carry an individual tool.

7—M1916 pistol cartridge pouch; the gunner's personal weapon was the 7.65mm Ruby automatic pistol. This pouch, very similar to but slightly longer than the standard rifle pouch, had an internal magazine holder.

8—ARS gasmask canister, a fluted cylinder originally issued painted horizon blue but during 1918 in khaki finish. The ARS ('*appareil respiratoire spécial*') was issued from November 1917; it was a copy of the German gasmask, with a filter cartridge screwing on to the front of the face mask.

9—M1892 haversack in light beige fabric.

10—M1877 two-litre water-bottle and slung mug.

11—M1914 semi-breeches, of standard cut but made in this example of a light, smooth, brushed material called '*ratine*', sometimes issued for summer clothing. Note the yellow infantry seam piping.

12—Horizon blue puttees.

13—M1917 ankle boots; the height of the ankle was increased by about 15mm that year, to give better support, but this modification made no real visible difference in practice.

14—M1915 *fusil-mitrailleur CSRG*. The 'Chauchat' was manufactured in haste by untried industrial processes (the maker, Gladiator, was in fact a bicycle manufacturer!) Nearly a quarter of a million were made, allowing its distribution throughout the French army from 1916, and also to the American Expeditionary Force. Unfortunately it used the 8mm Lebel cartridge, for ease of supply; and this rimmed round, quite unsuitable for the smooth feeding of automatic weapons, caused chronic stoppages. It was the cartridge shape that dictated the semi-circular design of the magazine.
François Vauvillier

GERMAN INFANTRYMAN, WESTERN FRONT, OCTOBER 1918

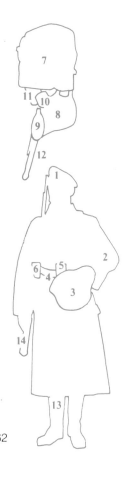

In the spring of 1918 Germany launched a last great offensive in the West, and by the use of surprise and of new, flexible tactics succeeded in making serious gains before Amiens and on the Marne. However, by July this offensive had been brought to a halt thanks to superhuman efforts by the French and British armies, and particularly to the fresh divisions of the American Expeditionary Force, which went on to the attack for the first time in May 1918. The German armies which were bled white in these summer battles were composed more of adolescents of the classes of 1919 and 1920 than of seasoned veterans. In his appearance, too, the soldier of late 1918 bore little resemblance to the infantryman of 1914; only his field cap and bayonet knot enlivened a uniform which had evolved under battle conditions, where inconspicuous drabness was synonymous with survival. The man illustrated, in full marching order for the long walk home, wears equipment of which many items are of *ersatz* industrial origin.

1—M1910 field cap in field grey cloth, its band and piping in the distinctive arm-of-service colour, here the red of the infantry. Two small pressed metal cockades are sewn to the front: that on the crown in the Imperial colours of black, white and red, and that on the band in the colours of the state of regimental origin, here the black and white of Prussia. This cap was only worn behind the lines after the first year or so of the war; in 1917 a drabber version with an all-arms green band was introduced, but the old type continued in use alongside it; a drab cloth strip was often fitted to cover the red band.

2—M1915 greatcoat in field grey, the large fall collar faced with green, as on the *Bluse*. It fastened with six large uniform buttons, and had two large flapped pockets in the sides, set at a slant. Although often sewn down, the shoulder straps were officially of detachable type, and bore the same white infantry piping and red unit number or monogram as on the *Bluse*.

3—M1916 helmet; here in monochrome grey, it was often painted with coloured camouflage patches by 1918. Here it is looped to the belt by its M1891 chinstrap.

4—M1895 blackened leather belt, the M1915 buckle plate painted grey, here of Prussian design with a crown and the motto 'Gott Mit Uns'.

5—Flashlight in black-painted metal, a non-regulation accessory sometimes seen fixed to a button by means of a leather tab, or, as here, looped to the belt.

6—M1909 cartridge pouches of *ersatz* manufacture, in vulcanised fibre. Like the leather originals, they carried four charger clips in each of the three pouches of each set, giving a total load of 120 rounds.

7—M1895 knapsack, here of simplified wartime manufacture in a greyish canvas. It accommodated reserve rations and changes of clothing. The M1892 tent section is rolled round the pack and fixed with leather straps. A wartime-made mess tin of M1910 design is strapped to the pack flap.

8—M1887 'breadbag' haversack in the greyish fabric often seen in equipment of wartime manufacture.

9—M1907 water bottle in enamelled iron, covered with recycled cloth—in this case, with brown corduroy. The attachment system had been simplified by this date to a single snap hook engaging with one of the rings mounted on the haversack.

10—M1893 mug; a green-enamelled metal was now used in place of aluminium for economy. One of its two handles is secured by the attachment loop of the haversack, inside which it was officially stowed.

11—M1917 *Lederschutzmaske* gasmask in proofed leather, in its grey-painted canister slung on a fabric strap.

12—Individual tool, here the M1887 portable entrenching spade, with the scabbard of the M1915 bayonet secured to it by a strap. Note the *Troddel* or bayonet knot in company colours.

13—Perhaps unusually for this date, this young man has a pair of the original knee boots of 1866 design, the tan leather blackened according to regulations.

14—M1898 Mauser rifle, 7.92mm calibre, with a wartime sling made of grey fabric with leather reinforcement at the ends.

63

UNITED STATES MARINE, WESTERN FRONT, 1918

Even by the Great War the US Marines already enjoyed a reputation as a crack corps specialising in overseas operations, and proud of their allegiance to the US Navy rather than the Army. It was natural that the Marines should provide an early contingent for the AEF, and the 'leathernecks' made up the 4th (Marine) Brigade of the 2nd Division (5th and 6th Marines, 6th Marine Machine Gun Battalion). If at first glance their uniforms and equipment appeared identical to those of the Army, there were in fact many small differences born of a fierce and exclusive *ésprit de corps*. These differences became less noticeable as convenience dictated the resupply of the Marine brigade from US Army stocks. Our subject is shown in the original 'forest green' uniform worn by reinforcements arriving directly from the USA. In the tradition of the USMC the Marines of the AEF played a major part in stopping the German offensive of May-June 1918 before Paris, and suffered heavy casualties.

1—M1918 'overseas cap' in olive drab; there was no 'forest green' version of this headgear. On the left front the USMC pinned the bronze badge of the Corps normally worn on the M1914 hat, the famous eagle, globe and anchor.

2—M1914 tunic in 'forest green' cloth. The stand collar bore no disc insignia in the Marines. It fastened with five large USMC buttons, and had four patch pockets with single-point buttoned flaps, the skirt pockets having 'bellows' or expanding gussets. Note pointed cuffs; and marksman's qualification badge above left breast pocket—a distinction achieved by some 70% of USMC effectives in 1918.

3—Flashlight of the type called a 'Liberty light', carried in a cloth pouch fixed by a tab to the buttonhole.

4—Light cotton ammunition bandolier, the five pockets each holding two five-round clips for the .30-06 Springfield rifle.

5—Cartridge belt, very similar to the US Army's M1910 item; differences included the USMC eagle, globe and anchor device on the press studs, and the stronger green shade of the fabric. Each of the ten pouches held two five-round clips.

6—M1910 first aid pouch, used by both Army and Marines; the markings on the metal box which protect the field dressing inside show that it was supplied by the Navy.

7—'Navy and Marine Corps model' Mills webbing suspenders, hooking to the upper eyelets of the belt.

8—M1910 canteen and carrier, differing from Army issue only in having press studs bearing the Corps badge, and being marked 'USMC' on the inside.

9—M1917 trench knife, with wooden grip, 'knuckle-duster' guard, and strong blade of triangular section.

10—M1905 bayonet in its M1910 fabric and leather scabbard. This was standard issue to all AEF infantry.

11—M1917 gasmask, copied from the British 'small box respirator' of the same date. Here it is carried slung across the body; in action the sling was shortened and slipped round the neck, holding the satchel high on the chest so that the mask could be donned at short notice.

12—M1917 helmet in manganese steel; the interior lining was in oilcloth, the chinstrap in brown leather. The example illustrated is painted in Marine 'forest green'.

13—M1914 trousers in 'forest green'. Cut straight, rather than as semi-breeches, these trousers had two slash side pockets and belt loops.

14—Puttees of olive drab cloth, identical to Army issue, though it is possible that 'forest green' examples may have existed.

15—M1917 ankle boots, common to the whole AEF.

16—M1903/05 Springfield rifle, .30-06 calibre, with 'no-buckle' web sling. The action is protected by a fabric weather cover fixed by press studs.

65

© Histoire & Collections/Laurent Mirouze

Printed in Singapore

This edition published
in Great Britain 1990 by
Windrow & Greene Ltd.
19A Floral Street
London WC2E 9DS

Reprinted 1995

British Library Cataloguing in Publication Data
Mirouze, Laurent
    World war one infantry in colour photographs -
    (Europa-militaria;3)
    1. Armies. Infantry, history
    I. Title II. Series
    326'.1'09

ISBN 1-872004-25-3

Acknowledgements:
The assembly of such a large number of original World
War I uniforms and items of equipment would have been
impossible without the generous collaboration of many
private collectors and museums throughout Europe. We
wish to express our gratitude to:
British Army Laurent Mirouze, and David Bardiaux,
curator of the Musée de la Targette, Neuville-St-Vaast
German Army Georges Bailly and Robert Bullock *French
Army* Laurent Mirouze, François Vauvillier and Jean
Pierre Verney *US Army* Georges Bailly *Italian & Austrian
Armies* Furio Lazzarini and Franco Mesturini *Belgian
Army* M. Jacobs, curator of the Musée Royal de l'Armée,
Brussels *Russian Army* Gérard Gorokhoff.

Photo credits:
Toni Bergamo (pp. 21, 33, 41, 43, 45); Stefan Ciejka (pp.
7, 13, 19, 27, 35, 49, 53, 59, 63); Laurent Mirouze (pp. 5,
37, 39, 51, 55, 65); François Vauvillier (pp. 9, 11, 15, 17,
23, 25, 29, 31, 47, 57, 61).